FAVORITE FAMILY RECIPES

ideals® FAVORITE

Family RECIPES

Edited by Peggy Schaefer

Ideals Publications
Nashville, Tennessee

ISBN 0-8249-5900-0

Published by Ideals Publications
A Guideposts Company
535 Metroplex Drive, Suite 250
Nashville, Tennessee 37211
www.idealsbooks.com

Designed by Marisa Jackson

Printed and bound in China

10 9 8 7 6 5 4 3 2 1

ACKNOWLEDGMENTS
Art: Page 7 by John Walter, © Ideals Publications; page 19 "Breakfast," 1914,
by Zinaida. Serebriakova, © 2006 Artists Rights Society (ARS), NY/ADAGP, Paris, from
Superstock; page 37 by Richard Hook, © Ideals Publications; page 53 © John Slobodnik;
page 73 by John Walter, © Ideals Publications; page 95 from The Bridgeman Art Library,
"Saying Grace," copyright © 1951 by the Norman Rockwell Family Entities, used by
permission of the Norman Rockwell Family Agency; page 115 "Suspense by Charles
Burton Barber (1845-1894), by permission of Fine Art Photographs, London; page 135
by V. Bocchino, © Swim Ink 2, LLC/CORBIS.

Table of Contents

Appetizers
7

Breads & Muffins
19

Vegetables & Side Dishes
37

Soups & Stews
53

Meats, Fish & Poultry
73

Casseroles & One-Dish Meals
95

Breakfasts & Brunches
115

Desserts
135

Appetizers

Cucumber-Cheese
  Sandwiches
Stuffed Celery
Stuffed Tiny Tomatoes
Chicken Liver Pâté
Pineapple Cheese Ball
Creamy Cheese Ball
Puffy Cheese Appetizers

Cheese & Spinach
  Appetizers
Sweet & Spicy Meatballs
Ham Pinwheels
Ham Deviled Eggs
Crabmeat Rounds
Crab-Stuffed Mushrooms

Cucumber-Cheese Sandwiches

1   8-ounce package cream cheese
1   8-ounce package Roquefort or blue cheese
½   cup mayonnaise
1   teaspoon Worcestershire sauce
    Thin white or wheat bread, crusts removed
    Garlic salt
1   medium cucumber, thinly sliced
1   cup chopped fresh chives

In a medium bowl, mix together cheeses, mayonnaise, and Worcestershire sauce until smooth. Cut bread slices into quarters. Spread cheese mixture on bread; top each with a light dusting of garlic salt, a cucumber slice, and a sprinkle of chives.

Makes 2 to 3 dozen

Stuffed Celery

1   4-ounce package blue cheese crumbles
1   cup plain yogurt or sour cream
¼   cup finely chopped green onions or chives
¼   teaspoon brandy extract, optional
1   bunch celery

In a small bowl, combine all ingredients except celery; chill until of spreading consistency. Cut celery into 2-inch pieces; fill with mixture. Serve cold.

Makes 3 to 4 dozen

Note: For variation, stuff celery with sharp cheese spread and sprinkle with chopped nuts.

Stuffed Tiny Tomatoes

½ pound potatoes, quartered
¾ cup chopped ripe olives, divided
½ cup chopped cucumber
1 hard-cooked egg, chopped
1 green onion, finely chopped
2 tablespoons mayonnaise
2 tablespoons sour cream
2 teaspoons Dijon-style mustard
1 teaspoon cider vinegar
1 teaspoon minced fresh dillweed,
    or ¼ teaspoon dried
Salt and black pepper to taste
About 70 cherry tomatoes

In a large saucepan, cook potatoes in boiling salted water until tender, about 20 minutes. Drain; cool, peel, and dice. In a mixing bowl, stir together potatoes, ½ cup chopped olives, cucumber, egg, onion, mayonnaise, sour cream, mustard, vinegar, and dill. Season to taste with salt and pepper; set aside. Cut a thin slice from stem end of each tomato. Scoop pulp and seeds from center with a small spoon or melon baller. Or cut a deep X from top of tomato almost to bottom and carefully pull tomato open; scoop out pulp and seeds. Fill tomatoes with potato salad mixture. Garnish tops with remaining chopped olives.

Makes about 70 stuffed tomatoes

Chicken Liver Pâté

½ pound chicken livers
3 tablespoons butter, divided
2 hard-cooked eggs
⅛ teaspoon black pepper
½ teaspoon Worcestershire sauce

2 tablespoons light cream
1 teaspoon salt
⅛ teaspoon celery salt
   Crackers

Cut livers into small pieces and sauté in 1 tablespoon butter in skillet until lightly brown. Chop livers and eggs into small pieces, using either a food chopper with fine blade or a masher. Add remaining ingredients and blend until smooth. Serve with crackers.

Makes about 1 cup

Pineapple Cheese Ball

2 8-ounce packages cream cheese, softened
½ cup crushed pineapple, drained
2 cups chopped pecans, divided
¼ cup finely chopped green pepper
2 tablespoons finely chopped onion
1 tablespoon seasoned salt
   Crackers

In a medium bowl, beat cream cheese until smooth. Stir in crushed pineapple, 1 cup pecans, green pepper, onion, and salt. Shape cheese mixture into a ball. Sprinkle remaining pecans on a piece of waxed paper; roll ball in pecans. Wrap in plastic wrap. Chill at least 6 hours before serving. Serve with crackers.

Makes 1 cheese ball

Creamy Cheese Ball

1 8-ounce package cream cheese, softened
1 8-ounce package blue cheese crumbles
½ cup flaked coconut, divided
1 teaspoon finely minced onion
1 teaspoon Worcestershire sauce
¼ cup chopped pecans
¼ cup finely chopped parsley
Crackers

In a medium bowl, combine cheeses; cream well. Blend in ⅓ cup coconut, onion, and Worcestershire sauce. Cover and chill at least 6 hours.

Before serving, mix remaining ingredients on a piece of waxed paper. Form cheese mixture into a ball and roll in the coconut, pecan, and parsley mixture until completely covered. Serve with crackers.

Makes 1 cheese ball

The tradition of serving appetizers began in ancient Athens. Whether called hors d'ouevres, starters, canapés, tapas, or antipasto, they are meant to whet the appetite for the forthcoming meal.

Mother's Kitchen

Puffy Cheese Appetizers

8 frozen pastry shells
1 egg, lightly beaten
1 tablespoon sesame seeds
½ cup finely chopped onion
1 tablespoon butter
¼ cup finely chopped fresh parsley
½ teaspoon salt
2 cups shredded Monterey jack cheese

Thaw pastry shells. Preheat oven to 450°F. On a lightly floured board, arrange 2 rows of 3 shells each, overlapping shells slightly. Roll and pat into a 10 x 14-inch rectangle. Carefully transfer to an ungreased 10 x 15-inch rimmed baking sheet. Prick bottom of pastry with a fork. Brush with egg; sprinkle with sesame seeds. Bake uncovered for 15 minutes. In a small skillet, sauté onion in butter until tender but not brown. Add parsley and salt; sauté 1 minute. Remove from heat; cool. Stir in cheese. Spoon parsley mixture over baked pastry to within ½ inch of the edge. Return to oven; bake uncovered until cheese is melted and pastry is brown, about 5 minutes. Cut into 2-inch squares.

Makes 3 dozen

Cheese & Spinach Appetizers

1   8-ounce package feta cheese, crumbled
1   8-ounce container small-curd cottage cheese
2   eggs, lightly beaten
1   10-ounce package frozen chopped spinach,
        thawed and thoroughly drained
¼   teaspoon salt
⅛   teaspoon garlic salt
⅛   teaspoon white pepper
½   pound phyllo or strudel dough
1   cup butter, melted

In a medium bowl, combine cheeses, eggs, spinach, salts, and pepper; blend well. Layer 5 sheets of dough, brushing each with melted butter. (While working, cover unused dough with a damp towel.) Spread filling thinly lengthwise over half of the layered dough. Roll up, jelly-roll style from long side with filling. Place rolls, seam sides down, on a large ungreased baking sheet. Brush generously with melted butter. Chill 15 minutes.

Preheat oven to 350°F. Use a sharp knife to score chilled dough in diagonal pieces about 1 inch apart, cutting only about ⅛ inch through the dough. Do not cut into filling. Bake 2 rolls at a time 35 to 40 minutes or until golden. Cool before cutting. For best results reheat before serving.

Note: To make triangles, place a single sheet of phyllo dough on a flat surface. Brush with melted butter. Cut lengthwise into 5 equal strips. Place 1 teaspoon filling on the end of each strip about 1½ inches from edge. Fold corner over filling to form a triangle. Repeat folding from left to right (as you would fold a flag) to end of strip. Brush with melted butter; chill 15 minutes. Bake 25 to 30 minutes, or until golden.

Makes about 5 dozen

In cooking,
as in all the arts,
simplicity is the sign
of perfection.

—CURNOSKY

Sweet & Spicy Meatballs

1 pound ground beef
½ cup dry bread crumbs
⅓ cup minced onion
¼ cup milk
1 egg
1 tablespoon chopped fresh parsley
1 teaspoon salt
⅛ teaspoon black pepper
½ teaspoon Worcestershire sauce
¼ cup vegetable oil
1 12-ounce bottle chili sauce
1 12-ounce jar grape jelly

In a large bowl, mix ground beef, bread crumbs, onion, milk, egg, and next four seasonings. Gently shape into 1-inch balls. In a large skillet, brown meatballs in oil. Remove meatballs to plate. Drain fat from skillet; add chili sauce and jelly. Heat until jelly is melted, stirring constantly. Return meatballs to skillet and stir until coated. Simmer 30 minutes, stirring occasionally. Serve hot in chafing dish.

Makes 5 dozen

Ham Pinwheels

1½ cups flour	8 thin slices cooked ham
1 cup grated Cheddar cheese	½ cup minced onion
½ cup butter, softened	¼ cup milk
2 tablespoons water	

Preheat oven to 450°F. In a large bowl, mix together flour, cheese, butter, and water until dough forms. Divide dough into 2 equal balls. On a lightly floured board, roll each ball into a 10 x 14-inch rectangle. Cut each rectangle into four 5 x 7-inch pieces. Place 1 slice of ham on each rectangle; sprinkle with minced onion. Roll up jelly-roll style from long side. Place each roll on an ungreased cookie sheet; brush with milk. Bake 10 to 12 minutes, or until golden brown. Remove from oven and cut each roll into 4 or 5 pinwheels. Serve hot.

Makes 3 dozen

Ham Deviled Eggs

6 eggs	1 tablespoon mustard
¼ cup finely chopped cooked ham	⅛ teaspoon onion powder
3 tablespoons mayonnaise	Paprika

Place eggs in saucepan and cover with water. Bring to a rapid boil. Reduce heat; simmer for 12 to 15 minutes. Remove pan from heat and pour off hot water. Fill pan with cold water and let eggs stand in water 5 minutes. Chill eggs in refrigerator.

When chilled, cut eggs in half; remove yolks and mash well in small bowl. Add ham, mayonnaise, mustard, and onion powder to yolks. Mix thoroughly. Spoon mixture into whites. Sprinkle with paprika.

Makes 12 egg halves

Crabmeat Rounds

1 6-ounce can crabmeat
1 3-ounce package cream cheese, softened
¼ cup mayonnaise
1 teaspoon minced onion
1 teaspoon salt
⅛ teaspoon black pepper
1 tablespoon chopped fresh parsley
   Toast rounds

In a medium bowl, combine all ingredients except toast rounds. Mound crabmeat mixture on toast; broil until bubbly.

Makes about 1 dozen

Crab-Stuffed Mushrooms

1 6-ounce can crabmeat, drained
3 green onions, chopped
¼ cup freshly grated Parmesan cheese
½ cup mayonnaise
12 jumbo mushroom caps, washed and dried
½ cup butter or margarine
   Grated Parmesan cheese

Preheat oven to 325°F. In a medium bowl, mix crabmeat, onion, and ¼ cup Parmesan cheese with mayonnaise; set aside. In a small skillet, lightly sauté mushroom caps in butter. Remove from pan and drain. Stuff caps with crabmeat mixture. Place in an ungreased shallow pan. Bake 5 minutes. Sprinkle caps with Parmesan cheese and broil for 3 minutes.

Makes 1 dozen

Breads & Muffins

Old-Fashioned Oatmeal Bread

Grandma's White Bread

Raisin Braid

Irish Soda Bread

Cheesy Surprise Bread

Sticky Pecan Rolls

Favorite Yeast Rolls

Cinnamon Coffee Round

Applesauce Nut Bread

Homestyle Gingerbread

Nutty Date Bread

Banana Muffins

Buttermilk Biscuits

Sweet Potato Biscuits

Country Corn Bread

Hush Puppies

Old-Fashioned Oatmeal Bread

  1 cup uncooked oatmeal
  1 cup milk, scalded
  ½ cup boiling water
  ⅓ cup shortening
  ½ cup packed brown sugar
  2 teaspoons salt
  2 packages active dry yeast
  ½ cup warm water
  5 cups sifted all-purpose flour

In a large bowl, mix oatmeal, milk, and boiling water. Add shortening, brown sugar, and salt. Let stand until lukewarm. In a small bowl, sprinkle yeast on ½ cup warm water; stir until dissolved. Stir into oatmeal mixture; add half the flour and mix until smooth. Gradually add remaining flour until dough is moderately stiff. Turn out on lightly floured board and knead 7 minutes. Place dough in greased bowl, turn once to grease lightly. Cover and let rise 1½ hours or until doubled in bulk.

Punch down; knead and shape into loaves. Place on a greased 10 x 15-inch baking sheet; cover and let rise until doubled in bulk. Preheat oven to 400°F. Bake 10 minutes. Reduce heat to 350°F and bake 40 minutes longer. Remove from pan and cool on wire rack.

Tip: To scald milk, pour milk into saucepan on low heat. Heat until milk is beginning to get hot with steam and small bubbles appearing around the edges, stirrng occasionally. Do not boil.

Makes 2 loaves

Grandma's White Bread

1 package active dry yeast
¼ cup lukewarm water
2 cups milk, scalded
¼ cup butter or margarine
2 tablespoons granulated sugar
2 teaspoons salt
6 cups all-purpose flour, divided

In a small bowl, sprinkle yeast over lukewarm water. Let stand for 5 minutes; stir to dissolve. In a large bowl, pour hot milk over butter, sugar, and salt. Cool to lukewarm; add yeast and 3 cups flour. Beat well. Add remaining flour and mix well. Turn out onto lightly floured board and knead until smooth and satiny, about 8 to 10 minutes. Place dough in greased bowl, turning once to grease lightly. Cover and let rise about 1½ hours or until doubled in bulk.

Punch down; cover and let rise for 30 minutes. Shape into 2 loaves and put in greased 9 x 5-inch loaf pans. Cover and let rise about 45 minutes, until doubled in bulk. Preheat oven to 400°F. Bake 35 minutes or until golden brown and bottom sounds hollow when tapped. Remove from pan and cool on wire rack.

Makes 2 loaves

Raisin Braid

3½ to 4 cups all-purpose flour
1 package active dry yeast
3 eggs
¼ cup granulated sugar
¼ teaspoon salt
1 cup whipping cream, lukewarm
1 teaspoon vanilla
1½ cups raisins
2 tablespoons milk

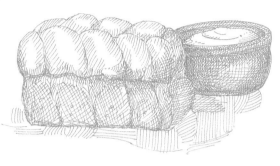

Sift 3½ cups flour into a large bowl. Sprinkle yeast onto flour; mix together. Separate one egg; set aside. Blend sugar, salt, cream, 2 eggs, egg white, and vanilla into flour mixture. If dough becomes sticky, add flour, but keep dough moderately soft. Place dough on lightly floured board and knead until smooth. Place dough in a greased bowl; turn once to grease lightly. Cover and let rise 1½ hours or until doubled in bulk.

Punch down dough. Turn out onto a lightly floured board and knead in raisins. Shape ⅔ of the dough into 3 rolls, each about 12 inches long. Braid the rolls together; place on a greased 10 x 15-inch baking sheet. In a small bowl, beat egg yolk and milk together. Press a hollow along the length of the braid with a rolling pin. Brush the hollow with egg yolk mixture. From the remaining dough, form 3 rolls, each about 10 inches long; braid them together. Place this braid atop the hollow of the larger braid; brush with egg yolk mixture. Cover and let rise 45 minutes or until doubled in bulk. Preheat oven to 375°F. Bake 35 minutes or until golden brown and bottom sounds hollow when tapped. Remove from pan and cool on wire rack.

Makes 1 braid

Irish Soda Bread

2 cups all-purpose flour
1 tablespoon granulated sugar
1½ teaspoons baking powder
1 teaspoon baking soda
¼ teaspoon salt
¼ cup butter or margarine, softened

¾ cup raisins
1½ teaspoons caraway seed, optional
1 cup buttermilk
1 egg
1 tablespoon water
2 tablespoons butter, melted

Preheat oven to 375°F. In a large bowl, sift together flour, sugar, baking powder, baking soda, and salt. Cut in butter with a fork or pastry blender until mixture resembles coarse meal. Stir in raisins and caraway seed. Add buttermilk; mix until dry ingredients are just moistened. Turn dough onto lightly floured board; knead for several minutes until smooth. Form dough into a round ball and place on a greased 10 x 15-inch baking sheet. Flatten ball until dough is about 1½ inches high. Beat egg and water together; brush top and sides with mixture. Cut a ½-inch deep cross in top of bread with sharp knife. Bake 30 to 40 minutes or until a wooden pick inserted in center comes out clean. Transfer to wire rack to cool; brush top with butter or margarine and cover with cloth.

Makes 1 round loaf

Cheesy Surprise Bread

1 package active dry yeast
1 teaspoon granulated sugar
1 cup lukewarm water, divided
3 to 3½ cups wheat flour
1 teaspoon salt
⅛ teaspoon black pepper
3 tablespoons vegetable oil
¾ cup Emmentaler cheese, cut into small cubes
⅓ cup Emmentaler cheese, cut into wedges
1 egg yolk
1 tablespoon water

In a small bowl, sprinkle yeast and sugar over ½ cup lukewarm water; set aside for 5 minutes. Sift flour into a large bowl; add salt and pepper. Pour in yeast mixture, remaining water, and oil. Mix well. If the dough is sticky, add a little flour, but keep dough moderately soft. Place dough on a lightly floured board and knead until smooth. Place dough in a greased bowl; turn once to grease lightly. Cover and let rise 1½ hours or until doubled in bulk.

Punch down dough. Place on pastry board and knead in the cubes of cheese until dough is smooth. Shape into a circle and place in an 8-inch greased soufflé dish. Insert cheese wedges into the dough. Cover and let rise 45 minutes or until doubled in bulk. In a small bowl, mix egg yolk and water. Brush top of bread with egg mixture. Preheat oven to 400°F. Bake 50 minutes or until bottom sounds hollow when tapped. Remove from dish and cool on wire rack.

Makes 1 loaf

Sticky Pecan Rolls

½ cup milk
4 tablespoons butter or margarine
⅓ cup granulated sugar
½ teaspoon salt
1 egg, lightly beaten
¼ cup lukewarm water
1 package active dry yeast

1 teaspoon granulated sugar
2½ to 3 cups all-purpose flour, divided
3 tablespoons butter, melted
1 teaspoon ground cinnamon
6 tablespoons granulated sugar
½ cup packed brown sugar
1 cup chopped pecans

In a small saucepan, scald milk. Add 4 tablespoons butter, ⅓ cup sugar, and salt; stir until butter melts. Cool to room temperature. Stir in egg; set aside. In a bowl, sprinkle yeast and 1 teaspoon sugar over water; let stand 5 minutes. In a large bowl, combine milk and yeast mixtures. Stir in 1 cup of the flour to make a soft batter. Gradually stir in remaining flour to make a stiff dough. Turn dough out onto lightly floured board. Knead until smooth and elastic, 8 to 10 minutes. Place dough in a greased bowl; turn once to grease lightly. Cover and let rise about 1½ hours or until doubled in bulk.

Roll out dough into a 16 x 8-inch rectangle. Brush top with 3 tablespoons melted butter. In a small bowl, combine cinnamon and 6 tablespoons granulated sugar. Sprinkle cinnamon mixture over dough. Roll up tightly from the long side. Cut into 12 slices. Generously grease a 12-cup muffin tin. Sprinkle brown sugar in muffin cups. Divide pecans among muffin cups. Place a piece of dough, cut side down, in each muffin cup. Cover and let rise 30 minutes. Preheat oven to 375°F. Bake 15 minutes or until golden. Invert rolls onto wire rack to cool.

Makes 1 dozen

Favorite Yeast Rolls

  1 cup milk
 ¼ cup granulated sugar
  1 teaspoon salt
 ⅓ cup shortening or vegetable oil
  2 packages active dry yeast
 ½ cup lukewarm water
  2 eggs, beaten
  5 cups sifted all-purpose flour

In a small saucepan, scald milk. Add sugar, salt, and shortening or oil; stir until dissolved. Cool to room temperature. In a bowl, sprinkle yeast over water; stir until dissolved and let stand 5 minutes. Add to milk mixture; add eggs. Gradually add flour; mix to a smooth, soft dough. Turn dough out onto lightly floured board; knead until smooth and satiny. Place dough in a greased bowl; turn once to grease lightly. Cover and let rise about 1½ hours or until doubled in bulk.

Punch down; shape into rounds or crescents. Place on 10 x 15-inch baking sheet. Cover and let rise 30 minutes or until doubled in bulk. Preheat oven to 425°F. Bake 15 to 20 minutes.

Makes 30 rolls

Bread is the king
of the table, and all else
is merely the court that
surrounds the king.

—LOUIS BROMFIELD

Cinnamon Coffee Round

　¾　cup granulated sugar
　6　tablespoons vegetable shortening
　1　egg
　2　cups all-purpose flour
　2　teaspoons baking powder
　1　teaspoon salt
　1　cup milk
　　Streusel Topping (recipe follows)

Preheat oven to 350°F. In a large bowl, cream sugar and shortening until light and fluffy. Beat in egg. In a separate bowl, sift together flour, baking powder, and salt. Alternately add flour mixture and milk to creamed mixture; blend well after each addition. Stir in half of the Streusel Topping. Spread batter in a greased 8-inch round baking pan. Smooth top of dough. Sprinkle with remaining Streusel Topping. Bake 30 to 35 minutes or until a wooden pick inserted in the center comes out clean. Serve warm.

Makes 6 servings

Streusel Topping

　½　cup granulated sugar
　2　tablespoons all-purpose flour
　1　tablespoon ground cinnamon
　2　tablespoons butter or margarine, melted
　¾　cup chopped nuts
　⅓　cup raisins, optional

In a small bowl, combine all ingredients; stir until blended.

Applesauce Nut Bread

　2　cups all-purpose flour
　¾　cup granulated sugar
　1　tablespoon baking powder
　1　teaspoon salt
　½　teaspoon baking soda
　½　teaspoon ground cinnamon
　1　egg, lightly beaten
　1　cup applesauce
　2　tablespoons vegetable
　　　shortening, melted
　1　cup chopped nuts

Preheat oven to 350°F. In a medium bowl, sift together flour, sugar, baking powder, salt, baking soda, and cinnamon; set aside. In a large bowl, combine egg, applesauce, and melted shortening; blend well. Gradually add flour mixture; blend well. Stir in nuts. Spread batter in a greased 9 x 5-inch loaf pan. Bake 1 hour or until a wooden pick inserted in the center comes out clean. Cool in pan 10 minutes. Invert onto a wire rack to cool completely.

Makes 1 loaf

Homestyle Gingerbread

1½ cups all-purpose flour
½ teaspoon baking powder
½ teaspoon baking soda
1 teaspoon salt
1½ teaspoons ginger
¾ teaspoon cinnamon

⅓ cup vegetable oil
½ cup packed brown sugar
1 egg, beaten
½ cup molasses
½ cup boiling water

Preheat oven to 350°F. In a large bowl, sift together first 6 ingredients. Make a well and add oil, then brown sugar and egg. In a small bowl, mix molasses and boiling water together; add to batter. Beat until smooth. Pour batter into a greased 8-inch square baking pan. Bake 35 to 40 minutes.

Makes 6 to 8 servings

Gingerbread can be baked in many forms— as a delicately spiced cake, a thick dark bread, or crisp flat cookies. And, of course, it can be pieced together to create a Christmas delight.

Nutty Date Bread

2 cups dates, chopped
1½ cups boiling water
1 cup granulated sugar
1 tablespoon butter, softened
1 tablespoon vanilla
1 egg
3 cups all-purpose flour
2 teaspoons baking soda
1 teaspoon salt
1 cup chopped pecans

Preheat oven to 400°F. In a small bowl, add dates to boiling water and set aside. In a large bowl, cream sugar, butter, and vanilla; add egg and mix well. In a separate bowl, sift together flour, baking soda, and salt. Add flour to creamed mixture; stir until just moistened. Drain dates well. Add dates and pecans to dough. Spread in a greased 9 x 5-inch loaf pan. Bake 15 minutes; turn down heat to 300°F and bake 1½ hours or until a wooden pick inserted in the center comes out clean. Let bread cool in pan 10 minutes. Invert onto wire rack and let cool completely.

Makes 1 loaf

Banana Muffins

    2   cups sifted all-purpose flour
   ⅓   cup granulated sugar
    2   teaspoons baking powder
  1½   teaspoons cinnamon
    1   teaspoon salt
    1   cup milk
    1   cup mashed ripe bananas
    1   egg, beaten
   ¼   cup shortening, melted
    1   tablespoon granulated sugar
   ¼   teaspoon cinnamon

Preheat oven to 400°F. In large a bowl, sift together flour, sugar, baking powder, cinnamon, and salt; set aside. In another bowl, combine milk, bananas, egg, and shortening. Add all at once to flour mixture, stirring only until dry ingredients are moistened; the batter will be lumpy. Fill greased muffin tins two-thirds full. Mix together remaining 1 tablespoon sugar and ¼ teaspoon cinnamon; sprinkle on top of each muffin. Bake 25 minutes.

Makes 1 dozen

Buttermilk Biscuits

2	cups all-purpose flour
2½	teaspoons baking powder
½	teaspoon baking soda
1	teaspoon salt
⅓	cup plus 2 teaspoons vegetable shortening
¾	cup buttermilk
2	tablespoons butter, melted

Preheat oven to 450°F. In a large bowl, sift together dry ingredients. Cut in shortening with a fork or pastry blender. Stir in buttermilk. Mix until dry ingredients are just moistened. Turn onto lightly floured board, turning several times to form a round ball. Pat dough into a circle, ½ to ¾ inch thick. Cut with a small floured glass or biscuit cutter and place on a greased 10 x 15-inch baking sheet. Brush tops with melted butter. Bake 12 to 15 minutes. Serve piping hot.

Makes 14 to 16 biscuits

Sweet Potato Biscuits

    1   teaspoon salt
    2   cups all-purpose flour
    4   teaspoons baking powder
    3   tablespoons butter
    1   cup mashed sweet potatoes
    ¾   cup milk

Preheat oven to 375°F. In a large bowl, sift together salt, flour, and baking powder. Cut in butter with fork or pastry blender until mixture resembles crumbs. Add sweet potatoes and enough milk to form dough. Turn out dough onto lightly floured board and roll out to ½-inch thickness. Cut biscuits with a small floured glass or biscuit cutter. Place on greased 10 x 15-inch baking sheet. Bake 14 minutes or until golden brown.

Makes 18 biscuits

When choosing fresh sweet potatoes, bigger may not be better. Look for small to medium potatoes, and store them in a cool, dry place.

Country Corn Bread

  1 cup all-purpose flour
3½ teaspoons baking powder
  1 teaspoon salt
1½ tablespoons granulated sugar
  1 cup yellow cornmeal
  2 eggs
  1 cup milk
 ¼ cup melted butter

Preheat oven to 400°F. In a large bowl, sift together dry ingredients. Make a small well in the center of the mixture. Add eggs and milk. Stir only until dry ingredients are moistened. Add melted butter. Pour batter into a greased 8-inch square baking pan. Bake 30 minutes or until lightly browned.

Makes 6 to 8 servings

Hush Puppies

  2 cups cornmeal
  1 tablespoon all-purpose flour
  1 teaspoon baking powder
  1 teaspoon salt
 ½ teaspoon baking soda
  3 tablespoons finely chopped onion, optional
  1 cup buttermilk
  1 egg, beaten

In a large bowl, combine dry ingredients. Add onion, buttermilk and egg. Mix well. Gently drop by tablespoonfuls into deep hot fat (375°F) and fry to a golden brown. Drain on absorbent paper. Serve very hot.

Makes about 2 dozen

Vegetables & Side Dishes

Carrot & Raisin Salad
Seven-Layer Salad
Deluxe Potato Salad
Texas Coleslaw
Zucchini & Tomato
   Casserole
Stewed Okra & Tomatoes
Creamy Asparagus Casserole
Creamed Spinach
Glazed Baby Carrots

Fresh Corn Pudding
Savory Black-Eyed Peas
Great Baked Beans
Oven-Roasted Potatoes
Scalloped Potatoes
Mashed Rutabagas
   & Potatoes
Sweet Potato Casserole
Swedish Red Cabbage
Baked Sauerkraut

Carrot & Raisin Salad

1½ cups water
¾ cup raisins
3 cups grated carrots
½ cup mayonnaise
¼ cup sour cream
½ teaspoon salt

2 tablespoons granulated sugar
1 teaspoon lemon juice
½ cup chopped walnuts, optional
½ cup diced pineapple, optional
Lettuce leaves

In a small saucepan, bring water to a boil. Add raisins; reduce heat and simmer 4 to 5 minutes. Drain and let cool. In a large bowl, mix carrots and raisins with mayonnaise and sour cream. Gently blend in salt, sugar, and lemon juice. Add walnuts and pineapple, if desired. Serve on crisp lettuce leaves.

Makes 4 to 6 servings

Seven-Layer Salad

1 head lettuce, shredded
½ cup chopped celery
½ cup chopped green onion
½ cup diced green pepper
1 10-ounce box frozen
    peas, cooked and drained

2 cups mayonnaise
2 tablespoons granulated sugar
8 strips bacon, cooked, drained,
    and crumbled
½ cup grated Cheddar cheese

In a large glass bowl, layer lettuce, celery, onion, green pepper, and peas. Spread mayonnaise to the edges of the bowl, sealing all. Sprinkle with sugar, then layer bacon and cheese. Cover tightly with plastic wrap and refrigerate until serving. May be prepared a day ahead.

Makes 6 to 8 servings

Deluxe Potato Salad

      8   medium new potatoes, skins on
      1   10.5-ounce can beef broth
      1   large red onion, finely chopped
    12   cherry tomatoes, halved
      2   or 3 canned artichoke hearts, drained and sliced
      4   hard-cooked eggs, diced
          Chopped fresh parsley
          Salt and black pepper
      1   cup mayonnaise

In a medium saucepan, boil potatoes in salted water until tender, about 20 minutes. Drain; let cool and slice. In a medium bowl, marinate potato slices in broth for 1 hour.

In a large bowl, combine onion, cherry tomatoes, artichoke hearts, eggs, a sprinkle of chopped parsley, and salt and pepper to taste. Just before serving, drain potatoes and add to vegetables. Stir in mayonnaise.

Makes 6 servings

Texas Coleslaw

1 medium head green cabbage, shredded
1 large green pepper, thinly sliced and chopped
1 large onion, thinly sliced and chopped
½ cup plus 1 tablespoon granulated sugar, divided
1 cup cider vinegar
1½ teaspoons celery seed
2 tablespoons dry mustard
1 cup vegetable oil

In a large bowl, combine cabbage, green pepper, and onion. Sprinkle with ½ cup sugar and toss; set aside. In a small saucepan, combine vinegar, 1 tablespoon sugar, celery seed, and dry mustard; bring to a boil. Remove from heat and stir in oil. Return to heat; bring to a boil. Remove from heat; pour mixture over cabbage. Toss several times. Cover and refrigerate overnight. Before serving, drain well. May be prepared a day ahead.

Makes 6 servings

There are many variations of coleslaw. Most are made with red or green cabbage and a mayonnaise- or vinegar-based dressing.

Zucchini & Tomato Casserole

    2 cups sliced zucchini
    1 cup thinly sliced onion
    2 small tomatoes, sliced
    ⅓ cup fine bread crumbs
       Salt and black pepper
    1 tomato, cut in wedges
    ½ cup grated Cheddar cheese

Preheat oven to 375°F. In a 1½-quart casserole, layer half each of the zucchini, onion, tomatoes, and bread crumbs; sprinkle with salt and pepper. Repeat layers. Top with tomato wedges. Cover and bake 1 hour. Uncover; sprinkle with cheese. Return to oven until cheese melts.

Makes 4 to 6 servings

Stewed Okra & Tomatoes

    1 small onion, chopped
    2 tablespoons vegetable oil
    1 10-ounce package frozen okra
    1 14.5-ounce can diced tomatoes
    ½ teaspoon salt
    ¼ teaspoon black pepper

In a medium saucepan, sauté onion in oil until lightly browned. Add remaining ingredients and cook, stirring occasionally to prevent sticking, until okra is tender and mixture thickens, about 10 to 15 minutes.

Makes 4 to 6 servings

Creamy Asparagus Casserole

1 pound fresh asparagus
2 tablespoons butter
2 tablespoons all-purpose flour
¾ teaspoon seasoned salt
¼ teaspoon black pepper
  Dash paprika
1 cup cream
½ cup shredded Swiss cheese
½ pound fresh mushrooms, sliced and lightly sautéed
½ cup minced celery
  Crushed crackers

Preheat oven to 350°F. Steam aparagus in steamer 5 minutes or in microwave 2 to 3 minutes, or until tender. Drain; set aside. In a medium saucepan, melt butter. Stir in flour and seasonings; cook until mixture bubbles. Add cream gradually, stirring until blended. Bring rapidly to a boil; cook and stir 1 to 2 minutes. Remove from heat; add cheese and stir until melted. Mix in mushrooms and celery. Arrange half the asparagus in the bottom of a greased shallow 1½-quart casserole. Pour sauce over asparagus and arrange the remaining asparagus on top. Sprinkle with cracker crumbs. Bake 25 minutes or until thoroughly heated. If desired, place under broiler until crumbs are browned.

Makes 6 servings

Creamed Spinach

1 large onion, chopped
4 tablespoons butter, divided
2 pounds fresh spinach, washed and dried well
2 tablespoons all-purpose flour
1 cup milk
½ teaspoon nutmeg
¼ teaspoon allspice
1 teaspoon salt
¼ teaspoon black pepper

In a large saucepan, sauté onion in 2 tablespoons butter until tender. Add spinach to onion and cook, covered, 3 to 5 minutes. Drain and chop spinach; set aside. Melt remaining butter in saucepan. Add flour; cook 1 to 2 minutes, stirring constantly. Slowly add milk and seasonings, stirring until smooth and somewhat thickened. Add spinach and cook, stirring, until heated through.

Makes 6 servings

Glazed Baby Carrots

2 bunches baby carrots, trimmed but whole
6 tablespoons butter
6 tablespoons packed brown sugar
½ teaspoon cinnamon or ginger

In a medium saucepan, boil carrots in a small amount of salted water 12 to 15 minutes or until tender. Drain thoroughly; set aside. In a large skillet, combine butter, brown sugar, and cinnamon or ginger. Cook over medium heat, stirring constantly, until well blended. Add carrots and cook over low heat, shaking the pan frequently to glaze carrots on all sides.

Makes 6 servings

Fresh Corn Pudding

1 tablespoon cornstarch
½ teaspoon granulated sugar
¾ teaspoon salt
⅛ teaspoon black pepper
1 cup milk, divided
3 eggs, lightly beaten
4 to 5 ears corn, husked and kernels scraped from cobs
     or 2½ cups frozen
⅓ cup minced onion
¼ cup minced green pepper
1 tablespoon butter or margarine

Preheat oven to 350°F. In a medium bowl, combine cornstarch, sugar, salt, and pepper. Stir in 2 tablespoons milk; blend until smooth. Stir in remaining milk. Blend in eggs and corn. In a small skillet, sauté onion and green pepper in 1 tablespoon butter until tender. Stir into corn mixture. Pour into a buttered 1½-quart casserole. Place casserole in a larger pan. Pour enough hot water into outer pan to reach the height of the corn mixture. Bake 1 hour or until knife inserted in the center comes out clean.

Makes 6 servings

Savory Black-Eyed Peas

   2 cups water
   1 16-ounce package frozen black-eyed peas
1½ cups chopped onion
   1 clove garlic, minced
   2 tablespoons vegetable oil
   1 8-ounce can tomato sauce
   1 teaspoon oregano
   1 teaspoon basil
  ⅛ teaspoon salt
  ⅛ teaspoon black pepper
   1 tablespoon lemon juice

In a large saucepan, bring water to a boil. Add frozen peas; bring to a boil. Reduce heat; cover and simmer 15 minutes. Drain, reserving ¾ cup cooking liquid; set aside. In a large skillet, sauté onion and garlic in oil until onion is golden. Stir in tomato sauce, oregano, basil, salt, and pepper. Simmer 5 minutes. Stir in peas, reserved liquid, and lemon juice. Cover and simmer, stirring often, about 30 minutes or until sauce is thick.

Makes 6 servings

*It's difficult to think
anything but pleasant
thoughts while eating
a homegrown tomato.*

—Lewis Grizzard

Great Baked Beans

    1 pound dry beans, such as Great Northern
           or Michigan Northern, sorted and rinsed
    5 cups warm water
1 1/2 teaspoons dry mustard
    2 teaspoons salt
  1/2 cup plus 2 tablespoons packed brown sugar
    2 tablespoons dark molasses
  1/2 pound salt pork, cut in 1-inch pieces
  1/2 pound boneless pork shoulder, cut in 1-inch pieces
    1 large onion, chopped

Soak beans in water overnight; drain, reserve soaking liquid. Place beans
in a slow-cooker. In a large bowl, combine mustard, salt, brown sugar,
and molasses. Stir in 5 cups reserved soaking liquid. Pour mixture over
beans. Add salt pork, pork shoulder, and onion. Bring to a boil; reduce
heat. Simmer, covered, 10 to 12 hours, stirring occasionally. Add more
water if beans become too dry during cooking.

Makes 8 servings

Oven-Roasted Potatoes

8 medium potatoes, peeled and quartered
1 small onion, minced
½ cup butter
Salt and black pepper

Preheat oven to 400°F. In a large saucepan, boil potatoes in salted water 15 minutes. While potatoes are boiling, in a small skillet, sauté onion in butter until golden brown. Drain potatoes; transfer to a shallow pan. Pour half of onion-butter mixture over potatoes. Bake 15 minutes; turn and coat with remaining onion-butter mixture. Bake until tender and golden brown. Season with salt and pepper.

Makes 6 to 8 servings

Scalloped Potatoes

4 large potatoes, peeled and cut into ⅛-inch slices
⅓ cup chopped onion
3 tablespoons butter
4½ teaspoons all-purpose flour
1½ teaspoons salt
⅛ teaspoon black pepper
2 cups milk

Preheat oven to 350°F. Layer potatoes in greased 1½-quart casserole. In a medium saucepan, sauté onion in 3 tablespoons butter until tender. Remove from heat; blend in flour, salt, and pepper. Slowly stir in milk. Return to medium heat and cook, stirring constantly, until mixture thickens slightly and comes to a boil. Pour mixture over potatoes. Bake, covered, 30 minutes. Uncover and bake 1 hour longer, or until potatoes are tender.

Makes 4 to 6 servings

Mashed Rutabagas & Potatoes

2 pounds rutabagas, peeled and sliced
3 medium potatoes, peeled and quartered
2 teaspoons salt
1 tablespoon granulated sugar
1 chicken bouillon cube
2 cups boiling water
¼ teaspoon black pepper
1 cup grated Cheddar cheese
2 tablespoons finely chopped onion
2 tablespoons butter
4 tablespoons fine bread crumbs

Place rutabagas, potatoes, salt, and sugar in a large saucepan. Dissolve bouillon cube in boiling water and pour over vegetables. Quickly bring to a boil; reduce heat and continue cooking until vegetables are tender, about 20 minutes. Drain and mash vegetables. Add pepper, cheese, and onion. Beat with mixer until fluffy; transfer mashed vegetables into casserole or baking dish. In a small skillet, melt butter. Add bread crumbs and cook, stirring, for 2 to 3 minutes. Top vegetables with buttered crumbs and broil until golden brown.

Makes 6 servings

Sweet Potato Casserole

8 medium sweet potatoes, peeled and quartered
¼ teaspoon nutmeg
½ teaspoon cinnamon
¼ teaspoon salt
4 tablespoons vegetable oil
⅓ cup granulated sugar
⅓ cup packed dark brown sugar
14 large marshmallows
¼ cup pecan halves

Preheat oven to 350°F. In a large saucepan, boil sweet potatoes for 20 minutes, or until tender. Drain; transfer to a large bowl and mash. Add remaining ingredients, except marshmallows and pecans, and blend. Spoon mixture into greased 9 x 13-inch casserole; sprinkle with pecan halves and cover with marshmallows. Bake 30 minutes.

Note: Casserole can be prepared ahead of time but should be baked immediately before serving.

Makes 6 to 8 servings

Swedish Red Cabbage

1 medium head red cabbage, shredded
¼ cup butter
3 tablespoons packed brown sugar
¼ cup chopped onion
2 firm tart apples, sliced
2 tablespoons vinegar
½ teaspoon caraway seeds
½ teaspoon salt
¼ teaspoon black pepper
½ cup grape juice

In a large skillet, sauté cabbage in butter over medium heat for about 5 minutes, stirring occasionally. Add brown sugar, onion, and apples; continue cooking for another 5 minutes. Add remaining ingredients; cover and simmer over low heat 30 to 35 minutes, stirring occasionally.

Makes 4 to 6 servings

Baked Sauerkraut

½ cup chopped onion
½ cup green pepper strips
2 tablespoons vegetable oil
1 8-ounce can pineapple slices, drained; reserve liquid
2 tablespoons cornstarch
1 cup beef bouillon
1 teaspoon soy sauce
2 teaspoons vinegar
¼ cup granulated sugar
⅛ teaspoon black pepper
½ teaspoon ground ginger
4 cups sauerkraut, drained

Preheat oven to 350°F. In a medium skillet, sauté onion and green pepper in oil until tender. In a small bowl, mix half the pineapple liquid with cornstarch; add to onion and green pepper. Gradually blend in remaining pineapple liquid and bouillon. Stir in soy sauce, vinegar, sugar, pepper, and ginger. Cook until thickened. Arrange half the sauerkraut and half the pineapple slices in the bottom of a 3½-quart casserole. Top with half the sauce. Add remaining sauerkraut and pineapple. Top with remaining sauce. Bake 30 minutes.

Makes 6 to 8 servings

Soups & Stews

Cream of Potato Soup
Favorite Onion Soup
Mixed Vegetable Soup
Lentil Soup
Hearty Bean Soup
Winter Vegetable Stew
Garden Skillet Stew
Brunswick Stew
Chicken Gumbo

Jambalaya
Chili con Carne
Mulligatawny Soup
Ham Bone Soup
Minestrone with Sausage
New Orleans Gumbo
Fish Stew
Classic Cioppino

Cream of Potato Soup

5   large potatoes, peeled and cubed
½   cup sliced carrots
6   slices bacon
1   cup chopped onion
1   cup sliced celery
1½ teaspoons salt
¼   teaspoon white pepper
2   cups milk
2   cups light cream or evaporated milk
    Shredded Cheddar cheese
    Parsley

In a large pot or saucepan, boil potatoes and carrots in lightly salted water about 15 minutes, or until tender. Drain; set aside. In a skillet, cook bacon until crisp. Drain, reserving two tablespoons bacon drippings; crumble bacon and set aside. Sauté onion and celery in reserved drippings. Add all ingredients, except cheese and parsley, to potatoes and carrots. Simmer 30 minutes. Garnish serving with Cheddar cheese and parsley.

Makes 4 servings

Favorite Onion Soup

4 cups thinly sliced onions
2 tablespoons vegetable oil
3 tablespoons butter
½ teaspoon salt
¼ teaspoon black pepper
¼ teaspoon thyme
3 tablespoons all-purpose flour
2 quarts beef broth
¼ cup rice wine vinegar
1 small loaf French bread, sliced into 8 pieces and toasted
8 slices Swiss cheese
Grated Parmesan cheese

In a large skillet, sauté onions in oil and butter until tender, but do not brown. Stir in salt, pepper, thyme, and flour; stir until flour is absorbed. Add broth and vinegar; simmer, partially covered, until onions are cooked, about 20 to 30 minutes. Pour soup into 8 individual crocks. Arrange toast and Swiss cheese on top of each. Sprinkle generously with Parmesan cheese. Broil until cheese is melted.

Makes 8 servings

Mixed Vegetable Soup

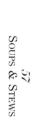

1 16-ounce package frozen mixed vegetables
1 small onion, diced
¼ cup butter or margarine
2 tablespoons all-purpose flour
2½ cups half-and-half or milk or combination
1 cup chicken broth
¼ cup chopped fresh parsley
1 teaspoon salt
⅛ teaspoon black pepper

Prepare vegetables according to package directions; drain and set aside. In a large saucepan, sauté onion in butter until onion is tender. Stir in flour; cook over medium heat 2 minutes or until bubbly, stirring constantly. Slowly stir in half-and-half. Cook until thickened, stirring constantly. Stir in broth. Add vegetables, parsley, salt, and pepper; heat through.

Makes 6 servings

Lentil Soup

2 cups lentils
4 slices bacon, cut into 1-inch pieces
2 cloves garlic, minced
1 large onion, chopped
1 large carrot, chopped
2 stalks celery, sliced
2 cups water
2 cups chicken or beef broth
2 tablespoons chopped fresh parsley
2 teaspoons salt
½ teaspoon black pepper
¼ teaspoon thyme
1 bay leaf
1 14.5-ounce can diced tomatoes

Place lentils in large pot or Dutch oven; add enough water to cover. Bring to a boil. Boil uncovered 2 minutes. Remove from heat. Cover and let stand 1 hour.

In skillet, fry bacon until limp; remove and drain, reserving drippings in skillet. Add garlic, onion, carrot, and celery to bacon drippings in skillet. Cook and stir over medium heat about 5 minutes or until celery is tender. Stir into lentils in pot. Stir in bacon and remaining ingredients, except tomatoes. Bring to a boil. Reduce heat; cover and simmer 1 hour (soup will be thick). Stir in tomatoes with liquid. Simmer uncovered 15 minutes. Remove bay leaf before serving.

Makes 6 servings

Hearty Bean Soup

- 1 pound dried red kidney beans
- 2 quarts water
- 2½ cups chopped onion
- 6 carrots, chopped
- 2 cups water
- 1 12-ounce can tomato paste

- 1 tablespoon chili powder
- 1 tablespoon salt
- 1½ teaspoons garlic salt
- ¼ teaspoon black pepper
- 12 ounces Provolone cheese, cubed

Rinse beans and place in large pot. Cover with 2 quarts water. Bring to a boil. Boil 2 minutes. Remove from heat. Cover and let stand 1 hour.

Uncover and bring to a boil. Reduce heat; cover and simmer 45 to 50 minutes or until beans are tender. Stir in onion, carrots, 2 cups water, tomato paste, and seasonings. Cover and simmer 30 to 35 minutes, or until carrots are tender. Stir cheese into hot soup just before serving.

Makes 8 servings

Kidney beans originated in Peru and were spread throughout South and Central America by Indian traders. They are an inexpensive source of protein and common in many soups and stews.

Winter Vegetable Stew

¼ cup chopped onion
1 clove garlic, crushed or minced
1 tablespoon vegetable oil
½ cup sliced carrot
1½ cups halved new potatoes
1½ cups apple juice
1 teaspoon crushed leaf basil
¼ teaspoon salt
⅛ teaspoon black pepper
2 cups coarsely chopped green cabbage
1 cup green beans, cut in 1½-inch pieces
1 cup sliced zucchini
1 cup chopped tomatoes
1 cup green pepper strips
1 tablespoon all-purpose flour
½ cup water

In a large saucepan, sauté onion and garlic in oil 1 minute. Add carrot, potatoes, apple juice, basil, salt, and pepper. Bring to a boil. Reduce heat; cover and simmer 15 minutes. Add cabbage, green beans, zucchini, tomatoes, and green pepper. Bring to a boil. Reduce heat; cover and simmer about 10 minutes or until vegetables are tender. In a small bowl, combine flour and water; blend until smooth. Slowly stir flour mixture into stew; cook about 1 minute or until thickened, stirring constantly.

Makes 10 to 12 servings

Garden Skillet Stew

1 pound chuck roast, cut into 1-inch cubes
2 tablespoons butter
1 tablespoon vegetable oil
1 cup diced onion
2 cups hot beef broth
2 teaspoons salt
¼ teaspoon black pepper
½ teaspoon dried dillweed
¼ teaspoon dried oregano
1 14.5-ounce can stewed tomatoes
2 tablespoons tomato paste
4 cups sliced green beans
4 cups fresh broccoli flowerets
1 cup chopped carrots

In large skillet or saucepan, brown meat evenly on all sides in butter and oil. Add onion during last few minutes of browning; continue cooking until onion is tender. Add broth, salt, pepper, dillweed, and oregano. Bring to a boil. Reduce heat; cover and simmer 45 minutes. Stir in tomatoes, tomato paste, and green beans. Bring to a boil. Reduce heat; cover and simmer 10 minutes. Add broccoli and carrots. Bring to a boil. Reduce heat; cover and simmer 15 minutes.

Makes 6 to 8 servings

Brunswick Stew

4 tablespoons bacon drippings

2 large onions, thinly sliced

3½ pounds chicken, cut into serving pieces

¼ teaspoon salt

¼ teaspoon black pepper

¼ teaspoon garlic powder

2 cups boiling water

4 tomatoes, peeled and chopped

¼ cup apple juice

1 teaspoon Worcestershire sauce

2 10-ounce packages frozen lima beans, thawed

1 10-ounce package frozen okra, thawed

1 10-ounce package frozen corn, thawed

3 tablespoons butter

½ cup seasoned dry bread crumbs

In large pot or Dutch oven, sauté onions in bacon drippings, until onions are tender. Add chicken, turning to brown all sides; add salt, pepper, and garlic powder. Add 2 cups boiling water, tomatoes, apple juice, and Worcestershire sauce. Simmer, partially covered, for 30 minutes. Add remaining ingredients except butter and bread crumbs. Simmer for 45 minutes or until tender, stirring occasionally. Stir butter into stew. Stir in bread crumbs and simmer 20 minutes.

Makes 6 servings

Chicken Gumbo

1 stewing hen (4 to 5 pounds)
1 teaspoon salt
1 stalk celery, cut in half
1 carrot, peeled and cut in half
1 medium onion, quartered
3 cups chopped celery
3 cups chopped carrots
2 cups diced onions
6 chicken bouillon cubes

Salt and black pepper
½ cup butter or margarine
½ cup all-purpose flour
1 14.5-ounce can stewed
  tomatoes
3 cups cooked rice
1 16-ounce package frozen okra,
  cooked and drained

In large pot or Dutch oven, combine chicken, salt, celery halves, carrot halves, and onion quarters. Add enough water to cover chicken. Bring to a boil. Reduce heat; cover and simmer 1½ to 2 hours or until chicken is very tender. Skim soup with spoon. Discard celery, onion, and carrot. Remove chicken from broth; skin and bone. Cut chicken into small pieces; place in refrigerator. Cool broth to room temperature, place in refrigerator until fat solidifies.

Skim fat from broth; return to stove. Bring to a boil; reduce heat. Add chopped celery, carrots, onions, and bouillon cubes. Season with salt and pepper to taste. Cover and simmer about 1 hour or until vegetables are tender. In a large saucepan, melt butter. Stir in flour. Cook over medium heat 3 to 4 minutes, stirring constantly. Gradually add about 2 cups hot broth, stirring with a wire whisk. Return mixture to remaining broth. Add tomatoes, rice, okra, and chicken. Heat through before serving.

Makes 8 to 10 servings

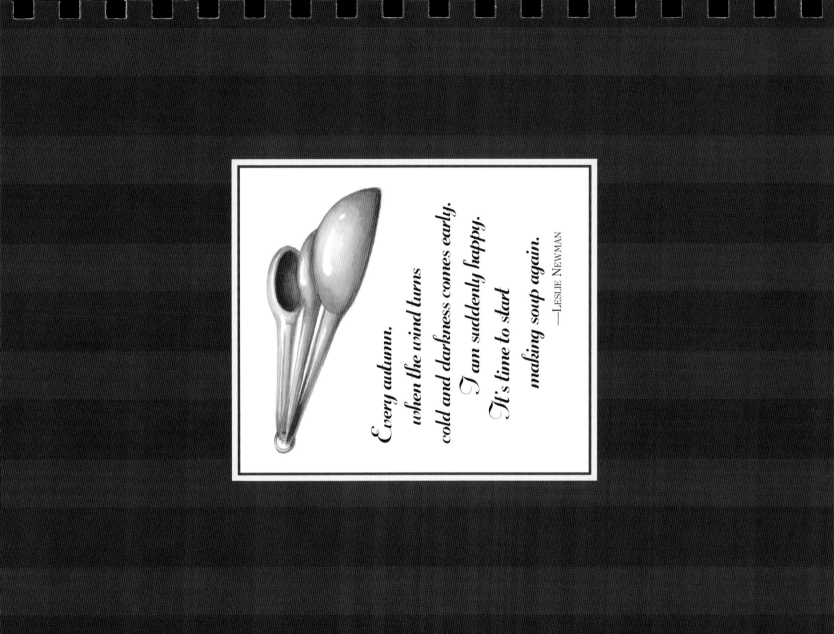

Every autumn,
when the wind turns
cold and darkness comes early,
I am suddenly happy.
It's time to start
making soup again.

—LESLIE NEWMAN

Jambalaya

1 cup cubed cooked ham
2 green onions, chopped
1 tablespoon butter or margarine
1 28-ounce can diced tomatoes
1 cup water
3/4 cup long-grain rice
1 bay leaf
1 teaspoon instant beef bouillon
   granules
1/2 teaspoon granulated sugar
   Dash hot pepper sauce
1 cup cooked shrimp, halved
1 medium green pepper, chopped

In a large saucepan, sauté ham and green onions in butter for 3 to 4 minutes or until onions are tender. Stir in tomatoes, water, rice, bay leaf, bouillon granules, sugar, and hot pepper sauce. Bring to a boil. Reduce heat; cover and simmer about 30 to 40 minutes or until rice is tender. Stir in shrimp and green pepper. Simmer uncovered for 6 to 8 minutes or until of desired consistency. Remove bay leaf before serving.

Makes 4 to 6 servings

Chili con Carne

1 pound ground beef
1 large onion, chopped
½ cup chopped celery
⅓ cup chopped green pepper
1 14.5-ounce can diced tomatoes
1 6-ounce can tomato paste
2 cups hot water
2 to 3 tablespoons chili powder
1 tablespoon salt
2 teaspoons granulated sugar
1 teaspoon garlic powder
¼ teaspoon ground cinnamon
2 16-ounce cans Mexican-style chili beans or red kidney beans
Chopped onion, optional
Shredded Monterey Jack or Cheddar cheese, optional

In a 3-quart saucepan, brown beef, onion, celery, and green pepper, stirring to break up meat. Stir in tomatoes with liquid, tomato paste, water, chili powder, salt, sugar, garlic powder, and cinnamon. Bring to a boil. Reduce heat; add beans. Cover and simmer 1½ hours, stirring occasionally. Serve with chopped onion and shredded cheese, if desired.

Makes 4 to 6 servings

Mulligatawny Soup

2 medium onions, quartered
4 tablespoons butter
4 large tomatoes, peeled and chopped
1 potato, peeled and sliced
2 cups cooked turkey
1½ quarts beef broth
1 teaspoon curry powder
½ teaspoon Worcestershire sauce
    Salt and black pepper
1 large apple, grated
    Cooked rice

Makes 6 servings

In large saucepan, sauté onion in butter until onion is tender. Stir in tomatoes, potato, turkey, broth, curry powder, and Worcestershire sauce. Bring to a boil. Reduce heat; simmer, partially covered, for 30 minutes, stirring occasionally. Season with salt and pepper to taste. Sprinkle with grated apple and serve with cooked rice.

Mulligatawny is an Indian soup and its name means "pepper water." In some variations, coconut is included in the soup.

Ham Bone Soup

1 to 3 trimmed ham bones*

4 quarts water

1 14.5-ounce can diced tomatoes

2 stalks celery, sliced

3 carrots, chopped

2 tablespoons barley

1 teaspoon dried parsley

3 peppercorns

Salt

½ small green cabbage, coarsely chopped

2 large potatoes, peeled and cubed

Place ham bone(s) in 2-gallon pot. Add water, tomatoes, celery, carrots, barley, parsley, peppercorns, and salt to taste. Bring to a boil. Reduce heat and simmer uncovered 2 hours. Add cabbage and potatoes; simmer 30 minutes. Remove peppercorns before serving.

*Do not trim ham bone too closely, as bits of ham add to the flavor of the soup.

Makes 8 to 10 servings

Minestrone with Sausage

½ pound bulk Italian sausage
1 small onion, chopped
1 carrot, chopped
2 cups water
1 14.5-ounce can tomatoes
1 15.8-ounce can Great Northern beans, drained
2 teaspoons instant beef bouillon granules
1 teaspoon salt
½ teaspoon crushed dried basil
⅛ teaspoon garlic powder
¾ cup small shell macaroni
1 small zucchini, chopped
  Grated Parmesan cheese

In large pot or Dutch oven, cook sausage, onion, and carrot over medium-high heat until meat is brown and vegetables are tender, stirring occasionally. Drain grease from pan. Add water, tomatoes with liquid, beans, bouillon granules, salt, basil, and garlic powder. Bring to a boil. Reduce heat; cover and simmer 20 minutes. Stir in macaroni; cover and simmer 5 minutes. Stir in zucchini; simmer uncovered about 5 minutes or until zucchini and macaroni are tender, stirring occasionally. Serve with Parmesan cheese.

Makes 6 servings

New Orleans Gumbo

¼ cup bacon drippings
5 tablespoons all-purpose flour
2 cloves garlic, minced
1 large onion, chopped
2 stalks celery, chopped
1 red bell pepper, chopped
2 tablespoons butter
1 quart chicken broth
1 28-ounce can crushed tomatoes
1 6-ounce can tomato paste
¼ teaspoon thyme
¼ teaspoon rosemary

¼ teaspoon oregano
2 bay leaves
1 teaspoon salt
¼ teaspoon black pepper
Dash hot pepper sauce
1½ pounds firm-fleshed fish fillets, cut into 1-inch pieces
¾ pound shrimp, peeled and deveined
1 10-ounce package frozen sliced okra, thawed and drained
½ teaspoon gumbo filé
4 cups cooked rice

In a small saucepan, heat bacon drippings over medium heat. Whisk in flour until it turns a deep rich brown; set aside. In large pot or Dutch oven, sauté garlic, onion, celery, and pepper in butter, stirring occasionally, until vegetables are tender. Stir in broth, tomatoes with liquid, tomato paste, seasonings, and flour mixture. Add hot pepper sauce to taste. Reduce heat; simmer, partially covered, about 20 minutes. Stir in fish, shrimp, and okra. Cover and simmer 10 minutes or until the shrimp is cooked. Remove pot from heat and stir in filé. (Do not reheat soup once the filé has been added.) Serve soup with hot rice.

Tip: Filé is a thickening agent that is found in many Creole recipes. Look for it in the spice or gourmet section of your supermarket.

Makes 8 servings

Fish Stew

1 quart fish stock, clam juice, or water
2 pounds firm-fleshed fish, cut into 1½-inch pieces
2 whole leeks, sliced
2 carrots, chopped
2 stalks celery, sliced
1 teaspoon salt
¼ teaspoon white pepper
¼ teaspoon thyme
2 bay leaves
4 tablespoons butter
4 tablespoons all-purpose flour
1 cup milk
1 egg yolk
1 cup heavy cream
Oyster crackers

In large pot or saucepan, heat fish stock over medium heat. Add fish, vegetables, and seasonings. Reduce heat; simmer uncovered 15 minutes or until vegetables are tender. In a small saucepan, melt butter; whisk in flour until absorbed. Stir in milk and egg yolk. Whisk in cream and simmer until thickened. Whisk mixture into fish stew; heat. Serve with oyster crackers.

Makes 6 servings

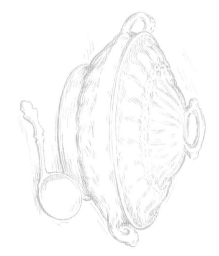

Classic Cioppino

1½ pounds assorted fish fillets, cut into 1-inch pieces
1 tablespoon lemon juice
2 potatoes, peeled and diced
1 cup chopped onion
¼ cup chopped celery
¼ cup chopped green pepper
¼ cup chopped fresh parsley
1 clove garlic, pressed
⅓ cup olive oil
1 14.5-ounce can diced tomatoes
1 8-ounce can tomato sauce
1 cup fish stock
1 teaspoon salt
½ teaspoon dried oregano
¼ teaspoon ground white pepper
1 cup chopped zucchini
2 6.5-ounce cans whole clams, drained

Sprinkle fillets with lemon juice; set aside. In large pot, sauté potatoes, onion, celery, green pepper, parsley, and garlic in oil until onion is translucent. Add tomatoes with liquid, tomato sauce, stock, salt, oregano, and pepper. Bring to a boil. Boil 5 minutes. Add fillets and zucchini to pot. Bring to a boil. Reduce heat and simmer uncovered 20 minutes or until fish flakes easily. Add clams and heat through, about 2 minutes. Serve immediately.

Makes 6 servings

Meats, Fish & Poultry

Saucy Meat Loaf
Stuffed Round Steak
Salisbury Steak Dinner
Shepherd's Pie
Lamb Spanakopita
Curried Lamb
Stuffed Grape Leaves
Pork Roast with
 Herb Stuffing
Oven-Barbecued Spareribs

Sunday Baked Ham
Old-Time Fish & Chips
Baked Stuffed Salmon
Tamale Cheese Pie
Chicken Fricassee
Chicken Pie
Southern Fried Chicken
Cornish Game Hens
 with Wild Rice

Saucy Meat Loaf

2 pounds ground beef
½ cup chopped green pepper
½ cup chopped celery
½ cup chopped onion
2 eggs, lightly beaten
1 package (1½ ounces) dry tomato soup mix
½ cup dry bread crumbs
½ cup milk
Salt and black pepper
1 15-ounce can tomato sauce
2 4-ounce cans mushroom stems and pieces, drained
⅔ cup water
2 tablespoons packed brown sugar

Preheat oven to 350°F. In a large bowl, combine ground beef, green pepper, celery, onion, eggs, soup mix, bread crumbs, milk, and salt and pepper to taste; mix only until blended. Shape into a loaf and transfer to a 9 x 13-inch baking dish. In a small bowl, combine tomato sauce, mushrooms, water, and brown sugar; blend well. Pour sauce over top of meat loaf. Bake, uncovered, 50 to 60 minutes or until meat loaf is no longer pink inside.

Makes 8 servings

Stuffed Round Steak

1 beef round steak (about 2½ pounds), fat trimmed
½ cup soy sauce
½ cup water
½ cup beef broth
1 tablespoon packed brown sugar
2 tablespoons lemon juice
2 tablespoons vegetable oil
¼ teaspoon hot pepper sauce
1 clove garlic, crushed
¼ teaspoon black pepper
  Bread or Rice Stuffing (recipes follow)
1 tablespoon cornstarch

Place steak between 2 sheets of plastic wrap or waxed paper. Pound with a mallet to about ⅛-inch thickness. Peel off plastic wrap or waxed paper. In a shallow glass baking dish, combine soy sauce, water, broth, brown sugar, lemon juice, oil, hot pepper sauce, garlic, and pepper; blend well. Place steak in marinade. Cover and refrigerate at least 2 hours, turning occasionally. Prepare Bread or Rice Stuffing.

Preheat oven to 350°F. Drain marinade from steak; reserve marinade. Pat steak dry with paper towels. Spoon stuffing onto steak, spreading to within ½ inch of all edges. Roll up lengthwise; secure with wooden picks and string. Return to baking dish with marinade. Cover and bake 1½ hours or until steak is tender, basting occasionally with marinade. Place stuffed steak roll on a cutting board. Remove wooden picks and string. In a small saucepan, dissolve cornstarch in a small amount of marinade. Stir in remaining marinade. Cook over low heat until slightly thickened, stirring constantly. Slice steak roll; arrange slices on a serving platter. Spoon sauce over steak slices.

Makes 8 to 10 servings

Bread Stuffing

3	tablespoons butter or margarine
¼	cup chopped onion
½	cup chopped celery
⅔	cup chopped water chestnuts
⅔	cup chopped bamboo shoots
½	cup chopped mushrooms
6	cups toasted white bread cubes or dry stuffing cubes
⅔	cup chicken broth
½	cup half-and-half
2	tablespoons chopped fresh parsley
1	teaspoon salt
¼	teaspoon black pepper
½	teaspoon crushed leaf sage
¼	teaspoon crushed leaf marjoram
¼	teaspoon ground thyme

In a large saucepan, melt butter. Add onion, celery, water chestnuts, bamboo shoots, and mushrooms; sauté until onion and celery are tender. Add remaining ingredients; blend well.

Rice Stuffing

¼	cup butter or margarine
½	cup chopped water chestnuts
½	cup chopped mushrooms
½	cup chopped celery
¼	cup chopped green onions
2½	cups cooked rice
1	cup bean sprouts, rinsed and drained
½	cup chicken broth
2	tablespoons chopped fresh parsley
2	tablespoons chopped pimiento
1	teaspoon salt
⅛	teaspoon black pepper
½	teaspoon ground ginger

In a large saucepan, melt butter. Add water chestnuts, mushrooms, celery, and green onions; sauté until celery is tender. Add remaining ingredients; blend well.

Salisbury Steak Dinner

1½ pounds ground beef
1 10.5-ounce can condensed
    onion soup, divided
½ cup fine bread crumbs
2 eggs, lightly beaten
6 tablespoons ketchup, divided
2 tablespoons grated Parmesan
    cheese, divided
½ teaspoon onion salt
⅛ teaspoon black pepper
1 tablespoon vegetable oil
¼ cup all-purpose flour
¼ cup beef broth
1 teaspoon Worcestershire sauce
1 teaspoon granulated sugar
½ teaspoon dry mustard
2 cups Mashed Potatoes
    (see recipe page 79)
2 tablespoons butter, melted
    Paprika

Preheat oven to 350°F. In a large bowl, combine beef, ¼ cup onion soup, bread crumbs, eggs, 2 tablespoons ketchup, 1 tablespoon Parmesan cheese, onion salt, and pepper. Shape into 6 oval patties. Heat oil in a large skillet. Dip patties lightly in flour; brown on both sides over medium heat. Drain off fat. Transfer patties to a 9 x 13-inch baking pan; set aside. In a small bowl, mix remaining onion soup, beef broth, remaining ketchup, Worcestershire sauce, sugar, and dry mustard. Pour mixture into skillet; heat, stirring to loosen browned bits. Pour over patties; cover and bake 25 minutes. Turn patties; cover and bake an additional 20 minutes. While patties are cooking, prepare mashed potatoes. Remove cover; drop large spoonfuls of mashed potatoes around edges of pan. Brush potatoes with butter; sprinkle with remaining Parmesan cheese and paprika. Bake, uncovered, an additional 20 minutes.

Makes 4 to 6 servings

78

Shepherd's Pie

2 cups Mashed Potatoes (recipe follows)
1 to 2 small onions, chopped
2 tablespoons vegetable oil
2 cups cubed cooked roast beef, lamb, or pork
1 tablespoon all-purpose flour
2½ cups canned or bottled beef gravy
Salt and pepper
1 cup carrots, cooked and quartered
1 cup frozen or canned peas, cooked and drained
1 egg, beaten

Prepare Mashed Potatoes. Preheat oven to 425°F. In a large skillet, sauté onions in oil until tender. In a medium bowl, lightly roll meat in flour until coated. Add meat to skillet and brown on all sides. Add gravy. Season to taste with salt and pepper. Transfer meat mixture to a greased 1½-quart casserole. Layer carrots and peas on top of meat. Fold egg into mashed potatoes; arrange in ring on top of meat. Bake 15 to 20 minutes, until gravy bubbles and potato ring is light golden brown.

Makes 4 servings

Mashed Potatoes

4 medium potatoes, peeled and quartered
¾ cup hot milk
¼ cup butter
1 teaspoon salt
Black pepper

In a large saucepan, boil potatoes in salted water 15 minutes, or until tender. Drain potatoes and return to pan; mash. Add milk and butter to potatoes; beat until well-blended. Season with salt and pepper to taste.

Lamb Spanakopita

½ pound ground lamb
2 tablespoons butter
1 small onion, chopped
¼ cup minced scallions
2 10-ounce packages frozen, chopped spinach, thawed and thoroughly drained
2 tablespoons minced fresh parsley
1 teaspoon dried dill weed
1 teaspoon salt
¼ teaspoon black pepper
¼ cup milk
¼ pound feta cheese, coarsely crumbled
3 eggs, lightly beaten
1 cup butter, melted
½ pound phyllo pastry

Preheat oven to 350°F. In a large skillet, brown lamb, stirring to break up meat. Remove to paper towels to drain fat. Discard any remaining fat in skillet. Melt 2 tablespoons butter in skillet; sauté onion and scallions until golden brown. Add spinach and seasonings; toss lightly. Remove from heat; add milk. In a medium bowl, combine feta cheese with eggs. Add to spinach mixture; mix well. Use a pastry brush to coat bottom and sides of a 9 x 13-inch baking dish with melted butter. Layer with 8 sheets of phyllo, brushing each sheet with melted butter. Do not trim overhanging sections. Pour in spinach mixture. Crumble lamb over top of spinach. Fold overhanging phyllo back over filling. Top with 8 sheets of phyllo, brushing each sheet with butter. Brush top with butter. Score into squares or diamonds. Bake 45 minutes. Let stand 10 minutes before serving.

Makes 8 servings

Curried Lamb

2 pounds ground lamb
2 slices raisin bread, trimmed of crusts and torn into pieces
1 apple, diced
½ cup milk
1 tablespoon curry powder
1 teaspoon salt
½ teaspoon black pepper
1 tablespoon vegetable oil
1 tablespoon all-purpose flour
½ to ¾ cup chicken broth
Prepared white rice
Optional condiments

In a large bowl, combine lamb, bread, apple, milk, and seasonings. Form into 2-inch balls. Press to flatten slightly. In a large skillet, brown meat patties in oil on all sides. Remove from pan; drain all but 1 tablespoon fat. Whisk in flour to make a smooth paste. Slowly add chicken broth. Cook and stir until smooth. Return patties to sauce; bring to a boil. Reduce heat and simmer over medium heat about 5 minutes, or until patties are cooked through. Serve with rice and condiments such as snipped green onions, chopped hard-cooked eggs, coconut, chopped peanuts or almonds, raisins, chopped green pepper, chutney. Use three or four condiments—some sweet, some salty, some fruity.

Makes 6 to 8 servings

Variation: Meat patties can be browned with no extra fat by placing on a lightly greased baking sheet and baking in 350°F oven for 15 minutes.

Stuffed Grape Leaves

1 tablespoon salt
1 1-pint jar grape leaves
2 pounds ground lamb
1 onion, chopped
1 clove garlic, minced
2 teaspoons salt
½ teaspoon black pepper
½ cup uncooked rice
½ cup chopped fresh parsley
1½ cups water
4 tablespoons butter
Lemon Sauce (recipe follows)

In a medium saucepan, bring 1 quart water to a boil. Add 1 tablespoon salt and grape leaves. Return to a boil; cover and cook for 10 minutes, separating leaves with a fork. Remove from heat and drain; set aside. In a large bowl, combine lamb and remaining ingredients, except butter and Lemon Sauce; mix well. Spoon 1 teaspoon of meat mixture onto the rough side of each grape leaf; roll up. Fill all leaves and place in a large pot, one layer on top of another. Dot top with butter. Cover and simmer for 1½ hours. Drain and reserve liquid; keep rolls in pot. Prepare Lemon Sauce. Pour sauce over rolls in pot; lightly shake to distribute the sauce. Let stand 5 to 10 minutes before serving.

Makes 8 to 10 servings

Lemon Sauce

2 eggs
3 tablespoons lemon juice
Liquid from grape leaves, above

In a medium bowl, beat eggs until light and fluffy. Add lemon juice. Slowly add liquid from grape leaves, beating constantly.

The feeling of
friendship is like that of
being comfortably filled
with roast beef.

—SAMUEL JOHNSON

Pork Roast with Herb Stuffing

1 tablespoon lemon-pepper seasoning
1 teaspoon tarragon
1 teaspoon salt
1 6- to 8-pound bone-in pork center loin roast
    Herb Stuffing (recipe follows)
¼ cup honey
1 tablespoon lemon juice
    Fresh tarragon sprigs, optional
    Lemon slices, optional

Preheat oven to 350°F. In a small bowl, stir together lemon-pepper seasoning, tarragon, and salt. Rub seasonings into roast. Cut slits about 2 inches deep between ribs of roast, without cutting through to opposite side. Pack stuffing into slits. Place roast on rack in a shallow roasting pan. Place a piece of aluminum foil loosely over top of roast just to cover stuffing. Bake for 30 to 35 minutes per pound or until meat thermometer registers 165° to 170°F. Combine honey and lemon juice; brush over roast and stuffing 15 minutes before end of cooking time.

Let roast rest 15 minutes before carving to allow juices to set. Garnish with fresh tarragon sprigs and lemon slices, if desired.

Makes 10 to 14 servings

Herb Stuffing

½ cup butter or margarine
1 bunch green onions with tops, chopped
1 clove garlic, minced
½ cup sliced fresh mushrooms
8 ounces herb-seasoned stuffing
1 tablespoon chopped fresh parsley
1 teaspoon lemon-pepper seasoning
1 teaspoon tarragon
½ teaspoon salt
1 egg, beaten
½ cup water
2 tablespoons lemon juice

In a large skillet, melt butter over low heat. Add onions and garlic; sauté over medium-high heat for 3 to 5 minutes. Add mushrooms; continue to cook for 2 to 3 minutes, stirring occasionally. Combine remaining ingredients in a large bowl. Add cooked mixture and toss gently to mix.

Makes 4 cups

Oven-Barbecued Spareribs

1 onion, diced
1½ cups ketchup
2 tablespoons white vinegar
¼ teaspoon red pepper
¼ teaspoon chili powder
1 tablespoon Worcestershire sauce
1 clove garlic, minced
2 racks (about 3 pounds each) spareribs

Preheat oven to 325°F. In a small saucepan, mix all ingredients except spareribs. Bring to a boil; reduce heat and simmer 5 minutes. Place spareribs in a shallow baking pan; cover and bake 30 minutes. Drain off fat; turn ribs and bake 30 minutes longer. Drain off fat. Cover ribs with sauce; increase oven to 400°F. Bake spareribs uncovered, basting often, 45 minutes or until fork tender, very brown, and glazed.

Makes 4 to 5 servings

Sunday Baked Ham

½ fully-cooked bone-in ham (about 5 pounds)
1 8-ounce can jellied cranberry sauce
2 tablespoons thawed frozen orange juice concentrate
¼ cup packed brown sugar
1 tablespoon vinegar
Dash ground cloves
Whole cloves

Preheat oven to 325°F. Place ham on a rack in a roasting pan. Trim excess fat or tough rind from top of ham with a sharp knife, leaving ¼-inch layer of fat. Score fat in a diamond pattern. Bake uncovered 30 minutes. During last ten minutes, in a small saucepan, combine cranberry sauce, orange juice concentrate, brown sugar, vinegar, and ground cloves. Bring to a boil; reduce heat. Simmer 2 minutes, stirring constantly. Remove ham from oven. Insert cloves where points in scoring meet. Brush glaze on ham; return to oven. Bake 1 hour, brushing with glaze every 15 minutes. Let rest 10 minutes before slicing.

Makes 6 servings

Cloves are the dried flower buds of the clove tree. They have long been used for both medicinal and cooking purposes.

Old-Time Fish & Chips

2 cups all-purpose flour
2 eggs, separated
½ teaspoon salt
¼ cup plus 1 tablespoon milk
¼ cup plus 1 tablespoon water
1½ pounds medium to large potatoes,
    peeled and cut into ¼-inch slices
2 cups peanut or vegetable oil
2 pounds flounder, sole, or haddock fillets,
    cut into serving-sized pieces
    Malt vinegar
    Tartar sauce

In a large bowl, mix together flour, egg yolks, and salt. Beat in milk and water; stir until smooth. Set aside for 20 minutes. Rinse potatoes in cold water and pat dry. In a deep saucepan, heat oil to 375°F. Fry potatoes, a few at a time, until tender but not browned (about 4 minutes). Drain potatoes on paper towels; cover with waxed paper and set aside. Keep oil hot. In a medium bowl, beat egg whites until stiff; fold into batter. Dip fish into batter; fry in hot oil, a few pieces at a time, until golden brown, turning as necessary. Drain on paper towels; transfer to a platter and keep warm in a 300°F oven while finishing potatoes. Increase oil heat to 390°F. Return potatoes to oil, a few at a time, and fry until crisp and browned. Drain on paper towels and sprinkle lightly with salt. Serve fish and chips with malt vinegar and tartar sauce.

Makes 6 servings

Baked Stuffed Salmon

1 5- to 6-pound salmon fillet with skin
  Salt and black pepper
  Juice from ½ lemon
½ cup butter
2 large onions, cut into ¼-inch slices
2 green peppers, cut into thin strips
3 cloves garlic, minced
1 28-ounce can diced tomatoes
½ cup water
1 teaspoon oregano
1 teaspoon basil
1 large bay leaf
2 tablespoons butter

Preheat oven to 425°F. Rinse fish and pat dry; sprinkle skin and inside with salt, pepper, and lemon juice. Transfer to baking dish; set aside. In a small skillet, melt ½ cup butter; sauté onions, green peppers, and garlic until onion is tender. Add tomatoes, water, oregano, basil, bay leaf, and salt and pepper to taste. Bring to a rapid boil; remove from heat and allow to cool slightly. Cut a slit in the center of top side of fillet, forming pocket for tomato mixture. Stuff fillet with tomato mixture and skewer the opening. Pour any leftover tomato mixture over the fish and dot with 2 tablespoons butter. Bake 25 minutes or until fish flakes easily when tested with a fork. Baste fish every 5 minutes while baking.

Note: This recipe can also be prepared with trout.

Makes 6 servings

Tamale Cheese Pie

1 pound ground turkey
1 cup chopped onion
½ large green pepper, chopped
1 small clove garlic, minced
4 cups whole canned tomatoes
1 to 2 teaspoons chili powder
¾ teaspoon cumin
¾ teaspoon salt
Dash black pepper
Cornmeal Topping (recipe follows)
1 cup grated Cheddar cheese

Preheat oven to 375°F. In a large skillet, sauté turkey, onion, green pepper, and garlic until vegetables are tender. Add tomatoes with liquid and seasonings; simmer 20 minutes. Prepare Cornmeal Topping. Pour turkey mixture into 8 x 8-inch baking pan; cover with Cornmeal Topping. Bake uncovered 20 minutes. Top with Cheddar cheese; bake an additional 10 minutes.

Makes 4 servings

Cornmeal Topping

½ cup cornmeal
⅔ cup water
1 teaspoon baking powder
½ teaspoon salt

In a medium saucepan, combine all ingredients and cook over low heat until thickened. Cool slightly; roll out to an 8-inch square on lightly floured board.

Chicken Fricassee

2 3-pound fryers, cut in pieces
All-purpose flour
¾ cup butter or margarine, divided
2 stalks celery, sliced
2 medium onions, quartered
2 carrots, sliced
1½ teaspoons salt
¼ teaspoon black pepper
¼ teaspoon dried rosemary
4 cups chicken broth
4 tablespoons all-purpose flour
½ pound mushrooms, sliced and sautéed
2 cups light cream, scalded

Dredge chicken in flour. In a large skillet, melt ½ cup butter; brown chicken on both sides. Transfer chicken to a large pot. Add celery, onions, carrots, spices, and chicken broth. Simmer 45 minutes or until chicken is tender. In a small skillet, melt remaining ¼ cup butter; add 4 tablespoons flour and cook 1 to 2 minutes, stirring constantly. Add flour mixture to stock. Simmer 2 to 3 minutes; add mushrooms and light cream. Simmer 3 to 5 minutes more. Serve over rice.

Makes 8 servings

Chicken Pie

1 4-pound stewing chicken, cut in pieces
1½ quarts water
1 tablespoon chopped fresh parsley
1 cup sliced carrots
1 cup sliced celery
1 cup peas
1 medium onion, diced
1 potato, chopped
1 cup sliced mushrooms
1 cup sliced parsnips
2 teaspoons seasoned salt
3 tablespoons butter or margarine, melted
3 tablespoons all-purpose flour
Dough for 6 biscuits or 1 9-inch pie crust

Place chicken in a large pot; cover with 1½ quarts water and bring to a boil. Reduce heat; cover and simmer 1½ to 2 hours, or until tender. Remove chicken and cool. Preheat oven to 350°F. Add parsley, vegetables, and seasoned salt to chicken broth; simmer until vegetables are tender, about 20 to 25 minutes. In a small skillet, melt butter; add flour and cook 1 to 2 minutes, stirring constantly. Add flour mixture to broth; simmer 3 to 5 minutes, or until thickened. Remove meat from bones and discard bones. Cut chicken into large chunks and add to vegetables and broth. Transfer to a greased, large casserole; cover with biscuits or pie dough. Bake 20 minutes or until brown.

Makes 8 servings

Southern Fried Chicken

2 2½- to 3-pound frying chickens, cut into serving pieces
2 cups all-purpose flour
1 teaspoon salt
½ teaspoon black pepper
1 cup milk
   Vegetable shortening

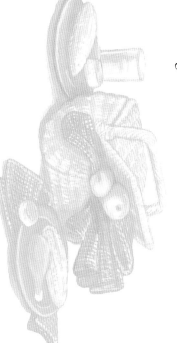

Clean chicken and pat dry. In a heavy paper or plastic bag, combine the flour and salt and pepper; shake to blend well. Pour the milk into a wide, shallow bowl; set aside. Melt enough shortening over low heat to come ⅛ to ¼ inch up the side of a large cast-iron skillet or heavy skillet. Heat oil to 325°F. Dip some of chicken pieces into milk; place in bag and shake to coat evenly. Arrange chicken in pan, skin side down; do not overcrowd. Put thighs in the center of pan, and breast and legs around the edge. The oil should come no more than halfway up the pan. Cook chicken until golden brown on each side, approximately 10 to 12 minutes per side. Internal temperature should be about 180°F on meat thermometer. Monitor oil temperature as well, making sure it does not exceed 325°F. When fully cooked, drain chicken on brown paper or paper towels. Continue with second batch, adding a little more shortening if needed. Transfer the chicken to a large platter for serving.

Makes 6 to 8 servings

Cornish Game Hens with Wild Rice

¼ pound fresh mushrooms, sliced
½ cup walnut halves
½ cup butter or margarine, divided
4 1-to 1¼-pound Cornish game hens
¾ cup wild rice
1 teaspoon dried minced onion
2 cups water
4 chicken bouillon cubes
  Garlic salt
  Black pepper

In a large skillet, lightly sauté mushrooms and walnuts in 2 tablespoons butter. Remove from skillet; set aside. Clean hens inside and out; pat dry. Truss legs to body of each hen. Add remaining butter to skillet; brown hens on all sides over medium heat. Reduce heat to low. Rinse rice; in a medium bowl, combine rice, onion, water, and bouillon cubes. Add rice mixture to pan; spread evenly under and around hens. Cover and cook 45 minutes or until hens are tender. Remove hens from skillet. Crisp hens, breast side up, 4 to 5 inches from broiler, if desired. Add mushrooms and walnuts to rice. Add garlic salt and black pepper to taste.

Makes 4 servings

Casseroles & One-Dish Meals

Homestyle Macaroni
& Cheese
One-Pot Lamb Roast
Yankee Pot Roast
Taco Casserole
Hungarian Goulash
Beef Stroganoff
Chicken & Dumplings
Chicken Noodle
Skillet Dinner

Chicken Paprika Casserole
Turkey Tetrazzini
Creamed Turkey with Popovers
Uncle Tony's Lasagna
Aunt Dessy's Moussaka
Stuffed Shells
Stuffed Green Peppers
Old-Fashioned
Stuffed Cabbage
Scalloped Potatoes & Ham

Homestyle Macaroni & Cheese

½ pound mostaccioli or macaroni
¼ cup butter
¼ cup all-purpose flour
2¼ cups milk
¼ cup minced onion
½ teaspoon salt
½ teaspoon dry mustard
3 cups shredded Cheddar cheese
Sliced pimiento-stuffed olives, optional
Tomato wedges, optional

Preheat oven to 350°F. Prepare mostaccioli according to package directions; drain and transfer to greased 2½-quart casserole dish. In a medium saucepan, melt butter over medium heat. Add flour; cook, stirring until bubbly. Add milk, onion, salt, and dry mustard. Stir until slightly thickened. Add cheese; stir until melted. Pour mixture over pasta. Bake 20 to 25 minutes. Let stand 5 minutes before serving. Garnish with pimiento-stuffed olive slices and tomato wedges, if desired.

Variation: Reduce cheese to 2 cups. Add 1 to 1½ cups diced cooked ham, chicken, or turkey to pasta before adding sauce.

Makes 4 to 6 servings

One-Pot Lamb Roast

1 lamb leg (shank half), about 4 pounds
2 onions, sliced thin
1 cup beef broth
1 cup water
2 teaspoons salt
1 teaspoon rosemary
½ teaspoon black pepper
6 large carrots, quartered
1½ cups fresh mushrooms, sliced

Preheat oven to 325°F. Place lamb in small roasting pan that has a lid. Add onions, broth, water, salt, rosemary, and pepper. Cover and bake 1 hour. Add carrots and mushrooms; cover and return to oven for another hour or until lamb and vegetables are tender. Remove lamb from oven and allow it to rest 10 minutes before carving. Cooking liquid may be skimmed of fat, strained, and served with lamb and vegetables, if desired.

Makes 4 servings

Yankee Pot Roast

1   3- to 4-pound boneless rolled rump roast or boneless chuck roast
2   tablespoons all-purpose flour
1   tablespoon vegetable oil
1   medium onion, chopped
1   10.5-ounce can condensed onion soup
½   cup beef broth
4   large potatoes, peeled and quartered
5   carrots, halved
    Few sprigs parsley, chopped

Dredge roast in flour. Heat oil in a large pot over medium-high heat. Brown roast on all sides. Add onion, soup, and broth; cover and simmer 3 hours. Turn once during cooking. Add potatoes, carrots, and parsley. Cover and simmer 40 to 50 minutes or until meat and vegetables are tender.

Makes 6 to 8 servings

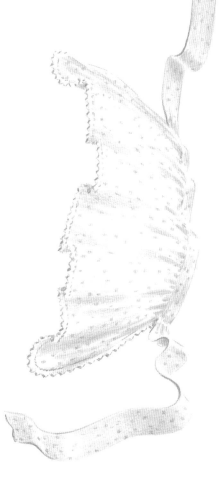

Taco Casserole

1½ pounds ground beef
 1 10-ounce can mild enchilada sauce
 2 15-ounce cans black-eyed peas, drained
 1 14.5-ounce can diced tomatoes
 1 teaspoon granulated sugar
 ½ teaspoon salt
 ⅛ teaspoon black pepper
 3 cups shredded Cheddar cheese
 1 head lettuce, shredded
 1 green pepper, cored and chopped
 1 medium onion, chopped
   Tortilla or corn chips, to garnish

Preheat oven to 350°F. In a 10-inch skillet, brown beef, stirring to break up meat. Drain; stir in next 6 ingredients; simmer, uncovered, 10 minutes. Layer half of mixture in 3-quart round casserole; sprinkle with half of cheese. In a medium bowl, mix lettuce, green pepper, and onion; arrange over cheese. Top with remaining meat mixture; sprinkle with remaining cheese. Bake 20 to 25 minutes. Garnish with warm chips.

Note: To warm chips, place in 300°F oven on a baking sheet until crispy, about 5 minutes.

Makes 6 servings

Hungarian Goulash

1 tablespoon vegetable oil

2 pounds lean boneless pork, cut in 1-inch cubes

2 large onions, chopped

1 clove garlic, minced

1⅓ cups water

1 tablespoon paprika

1 teaspoon caraway seed

1 teaspoon salt

⅛ teaspoon black pepper

1 27-ounce can sauerkraut, drained

1 cup sour cream

Chopped fresh parsley

In a large pot, heat oil over medium heat; brown pork on all sides. Add onions and garlic; sauté until onions are tender. Drain off fat; add next 6 ingredients. Bring to a boil; reduce heat. Cover and simmer 1 hour. Add sauerkraut; bring to a boil. Reduce heat; cover and simmer 30 minutes. Remove from heat; stir in sour cream and sprinkle with parsley.

Makes 6 servings

Paprika is a spice commonly found in Hungarian cooking. While mostly mild forms are found in the supermarket, stronger forms can be found in ethnic groceries.

Beef Stroganoff

1 pound sirloin steak
2 tablespoons butter or margarine
2 cups sliced fresh mushrooms
½ cup chopped onion
½ cup water
2 teaspoons Worcestershire sauce
1 teaspoon instant beef bouillon granules
½ teaspoon salt
1 cup sour cream
2 tablespoons all-purpose flour
8 ounces egg noodles
Paprika

Slice beef thinly across the grain into bite-sized strips. In a medium skillet, brown meat in butter over medium-high heat, stirring occasionally. Add mushrooms and onion; sauté 3 to 4 minutes or until onion is tender. Stir in water, Worcestershire sauce, bouillon granules, and salt; bring to a boil. In a small bowl, stir together sour cream and flour; stir into meat mixture. Cook over medium heat until thick and bubbly, stirring; cook and stir for 1 minute more. Prepare noodles according to package directions; drain. Serve over hot noodles; sprinkle with paprika.

Makes 6 servings

Chicken & Dumplings

1   4 to 5-pound stewing hen, cut up
3   to 4 sprigs fresh parsley
4   celery stalks with leaves, chopped
1   carrot, chopped
½   cup chopped onion
2   teaspoons salt
¼   teaspoon black pepper
    Dumplings

Makes 6 to 8 servings

Arrange chicken pieces in a large, heavy pot or casserole. Add vegetables and seasonings. Add enough cold water to just cover chicken. Cover and bring to a boil. Spoon off any foam. Reduce heat and simmer until tender, about 2½ to 3 hours. Add water as needed to keep chicken covered.

Fifteen minutes before chicken is done (make sure there is enough water to cover chicken), add dumplings as directed below.

Dumplings

1½ cups all-purpose flour
1   tablespoon baking powder
½   teaspoon salt
¾   cup milk
1   teaspoon minced parsley

In a large bowl, sift together flour, baking powder, and salt. Add milk and stir just until dry ingredients are moistened. Add parsley. Dip a teaspoon into hot chicken broth, then into dumpling batter; drop a spoonful of batter into chicken broth. Drop all dumplings in quickly. Cover and boil gently for 12 minutes; do not lift lid. Remove dumplings to platter and arrange pieces of chicken around them.

Chicken Noodle Skillet Dinner

- 2 tablespoons butter
- 1 tablespoon vegetable oil
- 1 3-pound broiler-fryer chicken, cut in pieces
- 1½ cups finely chopped celery
- 1 cup finely chopped onion
- ¼ cup shredded carrot
- 1 small clove garlic, pressed
- 1 teaspoon salt
- ¼ teaspoon white pepper
- ½ teaspoon dried tarragon leaves
- 1½ cups diced tomato
- ¼ cup tomato puree
- 1 chicken bouillon cube
- ½ cup water
- 8 ounces curly egg noodles
- Freshly grated Parmesan cheese

In a 10-inch skillet, heat butter and oil over medium heat. Brown chicken pieces, skin-side down until golden. Turn; brown other side. Remove from pan; set aside. Add celery, onion, carrot, garlic, salt, and pepper to pan drippings; sauté until celery and onion are tender. Add next 5 ingredients; bring to a boil. Reduce heat; simmer 3 minutes. Arrange chicken pieces over vegetables. Cover and simmer 30 minutes. While chicken is cooking, prepare noodles according to package directions. Drain noodles; arrange in center of large serving plate. Place chicken around noodles. Pour cooked vegetables and sauce over noodles. Sprinkle with Parmesan cheese; serve immediately.

Note: Blot chicken pieces with paper towels to avoid splatter when cooking.

Makes 4 servings

Chicken Paprika Casserole

8 ounces egg noodles

1 small onion, chopped

¼ cup butter

2 roasting chickens, about 2 pounds each, quartered

¼ cup all-purpose flour

1 teaspoon salt

½ teaspoon black pepper

1 tablespoon paprika

2 cups chicken broth

2 tablespoons tomato sauce

2 teaspoons Worcestershire sauce

2 cups sour cream

Preheat oven to 350°F. Prepare noodles according to package directions, cooking until barely tender. Drain and transfer to a 5-quart casserole. In a large skillet, sauté onion in ¼ cup butter. Remove onion; set aside. In same skillet, sauté chicken a few pieces at a time until lightly browned on both sides; add more butter if necessary. Arrange chicken on noodles in casserole. Whisk flour into drippings in skillet. Add salt, pepper, and paprika. Cook 1 or 2 minutes, stirring constantly. Slowly add chicken broth, stirring to blend; simmer until slightly reduced and thickened. Remove from heat, add tomato sauce, Worcestershire sauce, and sour cream; pour mixture over chicken. Bake 1½ hours.

Makes 6 to 8 servings

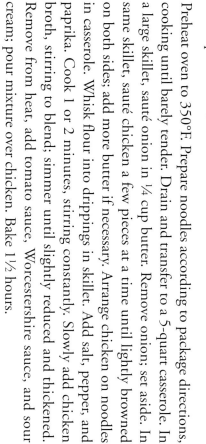

Turkey Tetrazzini

½ pound spaghetti, broken in half
½ pound sliced mushrooms
½ cup chopped onion
¼ cup butter
2 tablespoons all-purpose flour
2½ cups milk or half-and-half
¼ cup chicken broth
½ teaspoon salt
¼ teaspoon white pepper
2 tablespoons diced pimiento, drained
2 cups cooked cubed turkey
2 cups broccoli flowerets, cooked
1½ cups shredded brick or Muenster cheese

Preheat oven to 400°F. Prepare spaghetti according to package directions; drain. Arrange in a greased 9 x 13-inch baking pan, leaving a well in center. In a large saucepan, sauté mushrooms and onion in butter. Add flour; cook 1 to 2 minutes, stirring constantly. Add milk, broth, salt, and pepper; simmer, stirring, until slightly thickened. Add pimiento. Remove 1 cup sauce; pour over spaghetti in pan. Add turkey and broccoli to remaining sauce. Spoon into well in pan. Sprinkle with cheese; cover and bake 20 minutes.

Makes 6 servings

Creamed Turkey with Popovers

½	cup chopped celery	½	teaspoon salt
¾	cup sliced mushrooms	¼	teaspoon white pepper
⅓	cup thin green pepper strips	2	tablespoons diced pimiento,
3	tablespoons minced onion		drained
¼	cup butter	3	cups diced cooked white
3	tablespoons all-purpose flour		turkey meat
3	cups milk	8	Popovers (recipe follows)
¾	teaspoon poultry seasoning		

In a medium saucepan, sauté celery, mushrooms, green pepper, and onion in butter over medium heat 2 minutes. Add flour; cook 3 minutes. Add milk, stirring constantly. Add next 4 ingredients; cook over low heat 3 to 4 minutes. Add turkey; heat through. Spoon into Popovers.

Makes 8 servings

Popovers

3	eggs	1	cup all-purpose flour
1	cup milk	¾	teaspoon salt
1	tablespoon butter or	½	teaspoon granulated sugar
	margarine, melted		

Preheat oven to 375°F. Generously grease eight 5-ounce custard cups; place 4 along each long edge of jelly-roll pan. Set in oven 5 minutes while mixing batter. In a medium bowl, beat eggs until light and fluffy, using hand mixer or whisk. Add milk and butter; mix well. In a separate bowl, combine dry ingredients. Add to milk mixture; beat until smooth. Pour batter evenly into custard cups, using about ¼ cup batter for each custard cup. Cups should be about a third full. Bake 50 minutes. Cut a slit in side of each popover with sharp knife so steam can escape. Bake 10 minutes; immediately remove popovers from custard cups. Cut off tops and fill.

There is nothing better on a cold wintry day than a properly made pot pie.

—CRAIG CLAIBORNE

Uncle Tony's Lasagna

2 pounds ground beef
½ cup chopped onion
1 clove garlic, pressed
1 14.5-ounce can tomatoes
1 6-ounce can tomato paste
2 teaspoons salt, divided
1 tablespoon minced parsley
2 teaspoons dried oregano
1 teaspoon granulated sugar

1 teaspoon dried basil
⅛ teaspoon black pepper
9 lasagna noodles
1 egg
1 pound ricotta cheese
1 pound cottage cheese with chives
½ cup grated Parmesan cheese
1½ pounds thinly sliced
   mozzarella cheese

Preheat oven to 375°F. In a large skillet, brown beef with onion and garlic over medium heat, stirring to break up meat. Add tomatoes, tomato paste, 1½ teaspoons salt, parsley, oregano, sugar, basil, and pepper. Simmer, uncovered, 5 to 7 minutes, stirring occasionally. Prepare lasagna noodles according to package directions; drain. While noodles are cooking, beat egg in a small bowl; stir in ricotta and cottage cheeses, ¼ cup Parmesan cheese, and remaining ½ teaspoon salt. Arrange one-third of noodles in greased 9 x 13-inch baking pan. Spread with one-third of ricotta cheese mixture. Cover with one-fourth of mozzarella cheese slices. Top with one-third of meat sauce. Repeat layers twice. Arrange remaining mozzarella over meat sauce. Sprinkle remaining ¼ cup Parmesan cheese over top. Bake, uncovered, 40 minutes. Let stand 10 to 15 minutes before serving.

Makes 8 to 10 servings

Aunt Dessy's Moussaka

2 medium eggplants
Salt
All-purpose flour
1/3 cup olive oil
1 pound ground beef
2 medium onions, chopped
1 cup water
1 8-ounce can tomato sauce
1/2 cup minced parsley
1 clove garlic, minced
1 teaspoon salt
1/4 teaspoon black pepper
4 tablespoons bread crumbs, divided
2 tablespoons grated Parmesan cheese
Cream Sauce (recipe follows)

Preheat oven to 350°F. Peel eggplants, leaving some of the skin on in strips. Cut lengthwise into ¼-inch thick slices. Sprinkle with salt; allow to drain in colander 20 minutes. Rinse off salt and lightly squeeze slices to remove excess water. Dip eggplant slices in flour and place in greased broiler pan. Drizzle oil over top; broil about 5 minutes each side or until golden brown; set aside. In a large skillet, brown beef and onions, stirring to break up meat. Add water, tomato sauce, parsley, garlic, salt, and pepper. Simmer, uncovered, about 20 minutes. Remove from heat; stir in 2 tablespoons bread crumbs and cheese. Sprinkle remaining bread crumbs in bottom of greased 9 x 13-inch baking pan. Place half the eggplant slices in pan; spread meat mixture on top. Cover with remaining eggplant. Pour Cream Sauce on top. Bake 45 minutes or until golden brown. Cool slightly before cutting into squares.

Makes 6 servings

Cream Sauce

4 tablespoons butter
2 cups cold milk
3 tablespoons cornstarch
Dash salt
2 eggs

In a medium saucepan, stir butter, milk, and cornstarch over low heat until thickened, about 15 minutes. Stir in salt. Remove from heat; cool slightly. Beat eggs well; blend into sauce.

Stuffed Shells

18 jumbo pasta shells
1½ pounds ground beef
½ pound bulk Italian sausage
1 large onion, chopped
1 clove garlic, minced
3 cups shredded mozzarella cheese
½ cup Italian seasoned bread crumbs
¼ cup chopped parsley
1 egg, lightly beaten
Salt and black pepper
1 26-ounce jar spaghetti sauce
½ cup grated Parmesan cheese

Preheat oven to 400°F. Prepare pasta shells according to package instructions; drain and set aside. In a large skillet, brown ground beef and Italian sausage. Add onion and garlic; sauté until onion is tender. Drain off fat. Stir in mozzarella cheese, bread crumbs, parsley, egg, and salt and pepper to taste; blend well. Spoon about one-fourth of the spaghetti sauce over the bottom of a 9 x 13-inch baking dish. Fill pasta shells with meat mixture; arrange shells on top of sauce. Pour remaining spaghetti sauce over shells. Sprinkle Parmesan cheese on top. Bake 20 to 25 minutes or until bubbly.

Makes 6 to 8 servings

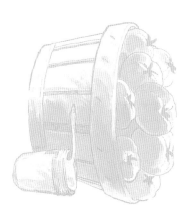

Stuffed Green Peppers

- 1 pound ground beef
- ½ cup chopped onion
- 1 clove garlic, pressed
- 1 teaspoon salt
- ¼ teaspoon black pepper
- ½ cup cooked rice
- ½ cup minced parsley
- 1 teaspoon dried dill weed
- 1 15-ounce can tomato sauce, divided
- 6 large green peppers, cut in half lengthwise, seeded
- ½ cup hot water
- 1 tablespoon butter
- 12 thin slices tomato
- Grated Parmesan cheese

Preheat oven to 450°F. In a 10-inch skillet, brown first 5 ingredients, stirring to break up meat. Add rice, parsley, dill weed and three-fourths of the tomato sauce; bring to a boil. Remove from heat. Fill peppers with mixture; place in a 9 x 13-inch baking pan. In a small bowl, mix remaining tomato sauce with hot water and butter. Pour around peppers in pan. Top each pepper with 1 tomato slice. Sprinkle with Parmesan cheese. Cover and bake 15 minutes. Reduce oven temperature to 350°F; bake 30 minutes. Uncover and bake an additional 10 to 15 minutes.

Makes 4 servings

Old-Fashioned Stuffed Cabbage

1 medium green cabbage, quartered vertically
1½ pounds ground beef
½ cup chopped onion
1 clove garlic, minced
1¼ teaspoons salt, divided
1 teaspoon dried oregano
¼ teaspoon black pepper
2 medium potatoes, peeled, quartered lengthwise, thinly sliced
½ cup grated carrots
½ cup bread crumbs
⅓ cup chopped parsley
1 8-ounce can tomato sauce, divided
1 cup shredded Cheddar cheese
1 tablespoon plus 1 teaspoon butter, divided
¾ cup water

Preheat oven to 350°F. Scoop out and discard center of each cabbage; set aside cabbage quarters. In a 10-inch skillet, brown beef with onion, garlic, 1 teaspoon salt, oregano, and pepper, stirring to break up meat. Remove from heat. Stir in potatoes, carrots, bread crumbs, parsley, ¾ cup tomato sauce, and cheese. Spoon into cabbage quarters; dot each with butter. Place in a 9 x 13-inch baking pan. In a small bowl, blend remaining tomato sauce, water, 1 tablespoon butter, and remaining salt; pour over cabbage. Cover tightly and bake 55 to 60 minutes.

Makes 4 servings

Scalloped Potatoes & Ham

6 medium potatoes, peeled and thinly sliced
¼ cup chopped onion
1 cup diced ham
1 10.5-ounce can condensed cream of mushroom soup
½ cup milk
1 teaspoon salt
⅛ teaspoon black pepper

Preheat oven to 375°F. In a large bowl, combine potatoes, onion, and ham; mix lightly. In a separate bowl, combine soup, milk, salt, and pepper; blend well. Pour over potato mixture, blending well. Transfer to a greased 9 x 13-inch baking pan. Bake, uncovered, 35 to 45 minutes, or until potatoes are tender.

Makes 8 servings

Canned soups offer a quick shortcut in many recipes. Cream of mushroom soup is one of the most popular flavors used for this purpose.

Breakfasts & Brunches

Buttermilk Pancakes
Homestyle Potato Pancakes
Golden Hash Browns
Easy Morning Omelet
South-of-the-Border Omelet
Poached Eggs Florentine
Eggs Benedict
Easy Egg & Sausage Casserole
Sausage Quiche

Onion & Bacon Quiche
Zucchini Frittata
Peachy-Plum Fritters
Old-Fashioned Doughnuts
Strawberry Cream Crepes
Pineapple Waldorf
Egg-Salad Stuffed Tomatoes
Gazpacho Macaroni Salad
Miniature Cream Puffs

Buttermilk Pancakes

2 eggs, beaten
2½ cups buttermilk
2½ cups all-purpose flour
1 teaspoon baking soda
2 teaspoons baking powder
1 teaspoon salt
2 tablespoons sugar
¼ cup butter, melted

In a large bowl, combine well-beaten eggs and buttermilk. In a separate bowl, sift together flour, baking soda, baking powder, salt, and sugar. Stir into egg mixture; blend until smooth. Stir in melted butter. Pour ¼ cup onto a hot, lightly greased griddle or skillet. Turn when bubbles begin to form on top and edges begin to brown. Continue cooking until bottom is brown. Repeat with remaining batter.

Variation: You can dress up pancakes by adding a little of your favorite fruits. After spooning batter onto the griddle, place a small amount of blueberries, raspberries, sliced strawberries, sliced peaches, or sliced nectarines onto the batter. Continue as above, turning after bubbles begin to form on batter and edges begin to brown.

Makes 20 to 24 medium-sized pancakes

Homestyle Potato Pancakes

1 cup ricotta cheese
1 egg
2 tablespoons all-purpose flour
1¾ cups peeled and shredded potatoes
1 cup diced ham
1 6-ounce jar sliced mushrooms, drained and chopped

In a large bowl, combine ricotta cheese, egg, and flour; blend well. Stir in potatoes, ham, and mushrooms. Drop heaping tablespoons of potato mixture onto a hot, lightly greased griddle or skillet. Brown pancakes over medium heat on one side about 3 minutes; turn and brown other side. Repeat with remaining batter. Serve warm.

Makes 2 dozen 3-inch pancakes

Golden Hash Browns

6 medium potatoes
2 tablespoons olive oil
2 tablespoons butter
1 medium onion, chopped
Salt and black pepper

In a large saucepan, parboil potatoes in salted water about 10 minutes. Drain; let cool. Dice or shred potatoes; set aside. In a large skillet, sauté onion in olive oil and butter over medium heat until caramelized, about 10 to 15 minutes. Mix potatoes into onions and season with salt and pepper. Cook over medium heat until potatoes are browned on bottom, about 5 to 7 minutes, shaking pan occasionally to prevent sticking. Turn once with spatula to prevent breaking up the potatoes; continue cooking until potatoes are tender and bottom is browned.

Makes 4 servings

Easy Morning Omelet

2 to 3 eggs
2 to 3 tablespoons water
⅛ teaspoon salt
   Dash black pepper
1 tablespoon butter
   Shredded cheese, optional
   Chopped salami, optional
   Chopped green pepper, optional
   Diced onion, optional
   Sliced mushrooms, optional
   Chopped ham, optional
   Chopped tomatoes, optional

In a medium bowl, blend eggs, water, salt, and pepper. In a 7- to 10-inch omelet pan or skillet, heat butter over medium-high heat until just hot enough to sizzle a drop of water. Pour in egg mixture. Mixture should immediately set at edge. With an inverted pancake turner, carefully push cooked portion at edge toward center and tilt pan as necessary so uncooked portion can reach hot pan surface. While top is still moist and creamy, add desired fillings.* With pancake turner, fold omelet in half or roll and slide from pan onto plate.

*It is better to fill omelet when it is slightly underdone; heat retained in eggs completes the cooking.

Makes 1 serving

South-of-the-Border Omelet

½ cup chopped onion
½ pound ground beef
⅛ teaspoon garlic powder
3 tablespoons butter, divided
½ cup chopped celery
½ cup chopped green pepper
2 teaspoons chili powder
¾ teaspoon salt, divided

1 cup chopped, seeded tomatoes
   with juice
1 cup shredded Cheddar cheese
4 eggs
2 tablespoons milk
½ cup sour cream or plain yogurt
2 tablespoons minced parsley

In a 10-inch skillet, sauté onion until tender. Add beef with garlic powder; cook until brown, stirring to break up meat. Drain off fat; add 1 tablespoon butter, celery, green pepper, chili powder, and ½ teaspoon salt. Cook over medium-low heat 3 minutes, stirring frequently. Stir in tomatoes; simmer until heated through. Stir in cheese until melted; set aside. In a small bowl, beat eggs, milk, and ¼ teaspoon salt. In a 9-inch omelet pan or skillet, melt remaining 2 tablespoons butter over medium heat. Pour in egg mixture; cook until light brown on bottom. Slide spatula around edge of egg mixture, lifting to let uncooked portion flow underneath. Cook until egg is partially set but not dry; heat retained in eggs completes the cooking. Fold omelet in half in pan; slide onto warm plate. Top with meat sauce and sour cream; sprinkle with parsley.

Makes 4 servings

Poached Eggs Florentine

1/4	cup butter or margarine
1/4	cup all-purpose flour
1/2	teaspoon salt
1/4	teaspoon hot pepper sauce
2	cups milk
1	10-ounce package frozen chopped spinach, thawed and drained

6	eggs
3	large tomatoes, halved
	Crumbled cooked bacon
	Grated Romano cheese

In a large skillet, melt butter. Blend in flour, salt, and hot pepper sauce; cook 2 minutes over low heat, stirring constantly. Slowly whisk in milk; cook until thickened, stirring constantly. Add spinach; heat to boiling. Carefully break eggs, one at a time, into spinach mixture; cover and cook over medium heat 5 to 8 minutes or until eggs are set. While eggs are cooking, broil tomato halves 3 to 5 minutes. Place one egg on each broiled tomato half; top with spinach sauce. Serve sprinkled with bacon and Romano cheese.

Makes 6 servings

Eggs are an incredibly versatile and useful form of protein. Most recipes are based on "large" eggs.

Eggs Benedict

4 eggs
2 English muffins, split
4 thin slices ham
8 canned asparagus spears or 8 fresh asparagus spears, cooked and drained
    Paprika
1 pitted ripe olive, cut in 4 thin slices
2 parsley sprigs
    Hollandaise Sauce (recipe below)

Make Hollandaise Sauce; set aside and keep warm.

Lightly grease a 10-inch skillet. Add enough water to fill skillet halfway; bring water to boil. Carefully break eggs, one at a time, into a small bowl. Gently slide each egg into water; do not overcrowd. Reduce heat and simmer uncovered 3 to 5 minutes, or until egg reaches desired firmness. Remove from water with slotted spoon. Toast and place 2 muffin halves on each plate; top each half with 1 slice ham and 2 asparagus spears. Place poached egg on top of each half. Top with Hollandaise Sauce; sprinkle with paprika. Garnish with 2 olive slices and parsley sprig on each serving.

Makes 2 servings

Hollandaise Sauce

¼ cup butter or margarine
2 egg yolks
2 tablespoons plain yogurt or fresh lemon juice
    Dash white pepper

In a small saucepan, combine first 3 ingredients. Cook, stirring, over low heat until mixture thickens. Stir in pepper.

Easy Egg & Sausage Casserole

1 small onion, chopped
1 red or green pepper, chopped
1 tablespoon butter
1 pound bulk lean sausage
6 slices bread, cubed
1½ cup grated Cheddar cheese, divided
6 eggs
2 cups milk
1 teaspoon salt
½ teaspoon black pepper

In a large skillet, sauté onion and red or green pepper in butter until tender. Remove from pan; set aside. Add sausage to skillet; brown, stirring with fork to break up sausage. Drain sausage. In a greased 9 x 13-inch baking pan, lightly toss sausage, onion, pepper, and bread cubes together. Sprinkle with 1 cup Cheddar cheese; set aside. In a large bowl, beat together eggs, milk, salt, and pepper. Pour over sausage mixture. Top with remaining cheese. Cover tightly and refrigerate 8 hours or overnight.

Preheat oven to 350°F. Uncover casserole and bake for 45 to 60 minutes, until eggs are set.

Variation: Substitute cooked ham for sausage in this recipe.

Makes 6 to 8 servings

Sausage Quiche

Basic Quiche Crust (recipe follows) or unbaked 9-inch pie shell

½ pound bulk pork sausage
¼ cup minced onion
1 cup shredded Swiss cheese
4 eggs
2 cups milk
½ teaspoon salt
Dash cayenne pepper

Preheat oven to 375°F. In a large skillet, brown sausage and onion, stirring to break up meat. Drain well on paper towels. Arrange sausage, onion, and cheese in unbaked quiche crust. In a large bowl, beat together 4 eggs, milk, salt, and pepper; pour over sausage mixture. Bake 30 to 40 minutes or until knife inserted in center comes out clean. Let stand 10 to 15 minutes before serving.

Makes 6 to 8 servings

Basic Quiche Crust

1½ cups all-purpose flour
½ teaspoon salt
½ cup shortening
1 egg, separated
¼ cup water

In a large bowl, stir flour and salt together. Cut shortening into flour with fork or pastry blender until pieces are size of small peas. In a separate bowl, beat egg yolk with water. Sprinkle into flour mixture a little at a time, mixing lightly with fork until dough begins to stick together. If necessary, add more water. Press together. Turn out dough onto lightly floured board and roll into 9-inch circle ⅛ inch thick. Gently fit into ungreased 9-inch pie pan. Trim pastry and flute edge of dough; brush pastry with lightly beaten egg white.

Makes one 9-inch crust

Onion & Bacon Quiche

1 pint dairy sour cream
3 eggs, lightly beaten
4 slices crisp bacon, crumbled
3 tablespoons chopped parsley
1 teaspoon Worcestershire sauce
1 teaspoon celery seed
1/4 teaspoon paprika
1/2 teaspoon salt
Dash white pepper
1 cup chopped onion
1/4 cup butter
2 tablespoons all-purpose flour
1/3 cup cooking sherry
1/4 cup grated Parmesan cheese
Paprika
Basic Quiche Crust (recipe on page 124) or unbaked 9-inch pie shell

Preheat oven to 350°F. In a large bowl, blend sour cream into eggs; stir in bacon, parsley, Worcestershire sauce, celery seed, paprika, salt, and pepper; set aside. In a large skillet, sauté onion in butter over low heat until tender. Stir in flour, mixing well; whisk in sherry. Add onion mixture to eggs and blend well. Pour into unbaked quiche crust. Sprinkle with Parmesan cheese and paprika. Bake 40 to 45 minutes or until filling is set. Let stand 15 minutes before serving.

Makes 6 to 8 servings

Zucchini Frittata

2 tablespoons butter, divided
1½ cups thin zucchini slices
1 small onion, chopped
⅛ teaspoon dried dill weed
⅛ teaspoon salt
⅛ teaspoon black pepper
4 eggs
½ cup shredded mozzarella cheese
½ cup plain yogurt
1 tablespoon minced chives

In an 8-inch skillet, melt 1 tablespoon butter. Sauté zucchini, onion, dill weed, salt, and pepper until onion is translucent. Remove from skillet; keep warm. Melt remaining butter in skillet over medium heat. In a small bowl, beat eggs lightly; pour into pan. Slide spatula around edge of pan, carefully lifting eggs so uncooked portion can flow underneath. Cook just until bottom is golden and eggs are partially set but not dry; heat retained in eggs completes the cooking. Slide eggs onto plate. Sprinkle cheese over eggs; top with zucchini mixture. Top with yogurt and sprinkle with chives. Serve immediately.

Note: If desired, frittata can be placed under broiler for a few minutes to brown the top.

Makes 2 servings

*Nothing stimulates
the practiced cook's
imagination like an egg.*

—IRMA ROMBAUER

Peachy-Plum Fritters

1½ cups all-purpose flour
¼ cup granulated sugar
2 teaspoons baking powder
½ teaspoon salt
½ to ¾ cup milk
1 egg, beaten
1 teaspoon vanilla extract
1 cup chopped fresh peaches
½ cup chopped fresh plums
¼ cup chopped nuts
Shortening or vegetable oil
Granulated or confectioners' sugar, optional

In a large bowl, stir together flour, sugar, baking powder, and salt; set aside. In a separate bowl, combine ½ cup milk, egg, vanilla; add to flour mixture, stirring until well blended. Stir in fruit and nuts. If necessary, stir in more milk to make a medium-thick batter. Heat shortening or oil (2 to 3 inches deep) in a heavy saucepan or electric skillet to 375°F on deep-fry thermometer. Gently drop batter by rounded tablespoonfuls into oil. Fry until golden brown, 3 to 4 minutes, turning once. Drain well on paper towels. Dust with granulated or confectioners' sugar, if desired; serve warm.

Makes 18 fritters

Old-Fashioned Doughnuts

2¼ cups all-purpose flour
½ teaspoon salt
1 tablespoon baking powder
½ teaspoon ground cinnamon
¼ teaspoon ground nutmeg
½ cup granulated sugar
1 egg
½ cup milk
1 teaspoon grated lemon zest
2 tablespoons butter, melted
Shortening or vegetable oil
Confectioners' sugar, optional

In a large bowl, sift together flour, salt, baking powder, spices, and sugar; set aside. In a separate bowl, beat egg; stir in milk, lemon zest, and melted butter. Blend into flour mixture, stirring until all flour is moistened. Cover and chill 15 minutes. Roll out dough to ½-inch thickness on a well-floured board. Cut with 3-inch floured doughnut cutter, dipping cutter into flour each time it is used. Heat shortening or oil (1½ to 2 inches deep) in a heavy saucepan or electric skillet to 375°F on deep-fry thermometer. Gently drop doughnuts into oil, 3 or 4 at a time. As they rise to surface, about 3 minutes, turn with fork or slotted spoon to brown other side. Remove doughnuts with slotted spoon. Drain well on paper towels. Serve plain or dust with confectioners' sugar.

Makes about 1 dozen

Strawberry Cream Crepes

3   eggs, beaten
1⅓ cups milk
3   tablespoons butter, melted
1   cup all-purpose flour
½   teaspoon salt
      Strawberry Cream Filling (recipe follows)

In a large bowl, combine eggs, milk, and butter; beat well. In a separate bowl, combine flour and salt. Gradually add flour mixture to egg mixture; beat until smooth. Chill at least 2 hours.

Heat a greased 6-inch skillet over medium-high heat until just hot enough to sizzle a drop of water. Place 2 tablespoons batter into skillet; rotate so batter covers bottom completely. Cook over medium to medium-high heat about 1 minute. When golden, gently turn to brown other side. Cook 30 seconds to 1 minute. Repeat for each crepe. Stack crepes on ovenproof plate or baking dish and keep in warm oven until all are ready to be filled.

Makes 16 to 18 crepes

Strawberry Cream Filling

½   cup granulated sugar
2   cups sliced fresh strawberries, divided
1   8-ounce package cream cheese, softened
¼   cup confectioners' sugar

In a small bowl, sprinkle granulated sugar over 1 cup strawberries; set aside. In a separate bowl, blend cream cheese and confectioners' sugar. Blend remaining 1 cup of the berries into cream cheese mixture. Spread about 1 tablespoon filling on each crepe; roll up. Serve with reserved sweetened strawberries.

Pineapple Waldorf

1 20-ounce can pineapple chunks, drained, reserving 1 tablespoon syrup
½ cup coarsely chopped pecans
½ cup diced celery
2 large apples, chopped
¾ cup crumbled blue cheese, divided
⅓ cup mayonnaise
3 cups salad greens
2 tablespoons lemon juice

In a large bowl, combine pineapple, pecans, celery, apples, and ½ cup blue cheese. Toss together lightly; set aside. In a separate bowl, blend pineapple syrup and mayonnaise. Add to pineapple mixture; toss lightly. Arrange mixture on greens on plates. Drizzle lemon juice on top. Garnish with remaining ¼ cup crumbled blue cheese.

Makes 6 servings

To pick a ripe pineapple, look
for one with little to no green.
And use your nose—a good
aroma indicates ripeness.

Egg-Salad Stuffed Tomatoes

4 large tomatoes
4 hard-cooked eggs
Mayonnaise
1 2.25-ounce can deviled ham
Salt and pepper
Lettuce
Parsley

Cut slice from stem end of each tomato. Scoop out pulp and set aside; turn tomatoes upside down to drain. Chop eggs; in a medium bowl, mix eggs with tomato pulp and enough mayonnaise to moisten mixture. Stir in ham; add salt and pepper to taste. Fill tomato shells with mixture. Serve on lettuce. Garnish with parsley.

Makes 4 servings

Gazpacho Macaroni Salad

2 cups uncooked macaroni
1 10-ounce package frozen peas
3 medium tomatoes, peeled and chopped
1 cup chopped celery
1 medium cucumber, diced
1 green pepper, chopped
5 green onions, thinly sliced
6 ounces salami, cubed

¼ cup chopped fresh parsley
⅓ cup olive oil
¼ cup red wine vinegar
1 teaspoon salt
½ teaspoon Worcestershire sauce
Dash hot pepper sauce, optional
1 clove garlic, pressed
Lettuce cups
Black olives, sliced

Prepare macaroni according to package instructions. Drain; rinse in cold water. Drain again; set aside. In a large bowl, cover peas with boiling water; let stand 2 to 3 minutes. Drain peas; add macaroni to bowl. Mix in tomatoes, celery, cucumber, green pepper, onions, salami, and parsley. In a cruet or small covered container, mix oil, vinegar, salt, Worcestershire sauce, hot pepper sauce, and garlic. Shake well. Pour over macaroni mixture; toss lightly. Serve in lettuce cups and garnish with olives.

Note: Salad may be mixed with dressing and chilled up to 3 hours. Toss again before serving.

Makes 6 to 8 servings

Miniature Cream Puffs

½ cup water
¼ cup butter or margarine
⅛ teaspoon salt
½ cup all-purpose flour
¼ cup finely grated Cheddar cheese, optional
2 eggs
Meat Filling (recipe follows)

In a medium saucepan, combine water and butter; bring to a boil. Add salt and flour all at once; stir quickly until mixture forms a ball. Remove from heat. Add cheese, if desired. Beat in 1 egg at a time, beating well until mixture is like velvet. Chill 1 hour.

Preheat oven to 400°F. Place by scant teaspoonful on a lightly greased 10 x 15-inch baking sheet; mound each with tip of spoon. Bake 15 to 18 minutes, until puffed and golden brown. Split cream puffs in half and fill with Meat Filling.

Makes about 4 to 5 dozen

Meat Filling

1½ cups chopped cooked chicken, shrimp, or crabmeat
2 tablespoons minced celery or water chestnuts
1 teaspoon minced onion
Seasoned salt to taste
3 to 4 tablespoons mayonnaise

In a medium bowl, combine all ingredients, mixing well.

Desserts

Glazed Fruit Tarts	Cola Cake
Perfect Peach Crisp	Holiday Chocolate Cake
Lemon Meringue Pie	Strawberry-Topped Cheesecake
Deep-Dish Strawberry-	Double-Decker Espresso Mousse
Rhubarb Pie	Cocoa Cream Puffs
Pecan Chess Pie	Chocolate Soufflé
Chocolate Bavarian Cream Pie	Apricot Linzer Cookies
Old-Fashioned Pound Cake	Hazelnut Macaroons
Great-Grandma's Raisin Cake	Almond Butter Cookies
Poppy Seed Cake	Pinwheel Cookies
Black Forest Cake	Favorite Brownies

Glazed Fruit Tarts

- 1   8-ounce package cream cheese, softened
- ½   cup granulated sugar
- 2   tablespoons cream or milk
- 2   tablespoons orange juice
- 1   teaspoon grated orange rind
- 24 baked 1¾-inch tart shells
- 1   pint strawberries, hulled, or raspberries or blueberries
       Glaze (recipe follows)

In a medium bowl, beat cream cheese, sugar, cream, orange juice, and orange rind until smooth. Fill shells ¾ full with mixture. Top with fruit of your choice; chill 15 to 20 minutes. Prepare Glaze; spoon over fruit. Chill at least 30 minutes. Store in refrigerator.

Makes 24 tarts

Glaze

- 1   tablespoon cornstarch
- ½   cup granulated sugar
- 1   cup fresh or frozen strawberries, raspberries, or blueberries,
       crushed (use same fruit as selected above)
- 1   teaspoon lemon juice

In a small saucepan, combine cornstarch and sugar; stir in crushed berries and lemon juice. Cook over medium heat until thickened and translucent; strain. Cool before spooning over tarts.

Perfect Peach Crisp

3 cups sliced fresh or drained canned peaches
1 tablespoon lemon juice
1 cup all-purpose flour
1 cup granulated sugar
½ teaspoon salt
1 egg, lightly beaten
6 tablespoons butter or margarine, melted
Ice cream, optional

Preheat oven to 375°F. Arrange peach slices in an 8 x 8-inch baking dish. Sprinkle with lemon juice. (Omit lemon juice if using canned peaches.) In a large bowl, sift together flour, sugar, and salt. Add egg; mix lightly with fork until crumbly. Sprinkle crumb mixture over peaches. Drizzle melted butter over top. Bake for 35 to 40 minutes or until topping is golden. Serve with ice cream, if desired.

Makes 6 servings

Lemon Meringue Pie

1 cup granulated sugar
6 tablespoons cornstarch
1½ cups water
½ cup lemon juice
2 teaspoons grated lemon rind
4 egg yolks, lightly beaten
3 tablespoons butter
1 9-inch baked pie crust
Meringue (recipe follows)

Preheat oven to 450°F. In a saucepan, combine sugar and cornstarch; mix thoroughly. Stir in water, lemon juice, lemon rind, and egg yolks. Simmer over low heat, whisking constantly, until mixture thickens and becomes translucent; remove from heat. Add butter; whisk until butter melts and mixture cools slightly. Pour into pie crust. Prepare Meringue and spread over filling, bringing to edge of crust. Bake 8 to 10 minutes or until peaks of meringue are golden.

Makes 6 to 8 servings

Meringue

4 egg whites, room temperature
½ teaspoon cream of tartar
¼ cup granulated sugar

In a large bowl, beat egg whites until foamy. Add cream of tartar and sugar, 1 tablespoon at a time, beating until stiff peaks form and mixture is glossy.

Deep-Dish Strawberry-Rhubarb Pie

3 cups ½-inch rhubarb pieces
2 cups sliced strawberries
1 tablespoon lemon juice
½ teaspoon vanilla extract
1½ cups plus 1 tablespoon
  granulated sugar, divided

3 tablespoons tapioca
2 tablespoons butter or margarine
  Pastry for 9-inch single pie crust

Preheat oven to 400°F. Spread fruits in an 8-inch square baking dish; sprinkle with lemon juice and vanilla. In a small bowl, combine 1½ cups sugar and tapioca; pour over fruit and mix gently. Dot with butter. Roll out pastry to a 9-inch square and place over fruit. Crimp at edge of pan to seal; cut 3 slits to vent steam. Sprinkle crust with 1 tablespoon sugar. Bake 45 to 50 minutes until crust is golden brown. Cool on rack.

Makes 6 to 8 servings

Pecan Chess Pie

½ cup butter or margarine
1½ cups granulated sugar
1 tablespoon cornmeal
3 eggs, lightly beaten
1 tablespoon lemon juice

1 teaspoon vanilla extract
1 cup pecan halves
½ cup toasted flaked coconut
1 9-inch unbaked pie crust

Preheat oven to 350°F. In a medium saucepan, melt butter; stir in sugar, cornmeal, eggs, lemon juice, and vanilla. Spread nuts and coconut in bottom of pie crust. Top with egg mixture; bake 50 to 60 minutes or until knife inserted in custard comes out clean. Cool on rack.

Note: To toast flaked coconut, spread coconut on baking sheet; bake at 325°F 10 minutes or until golden brown.

Makes 6 to 8 servings

Chocolate Bavarian Cream Pie

1 envelope unflavored gelatin
1¾ cups milk, divided
⅔ cup granulated sugar
6 tablespoons cocoa
1 tablespoon light corn syrup
2 tablespoons butter or margarine
¾ teaspoon vanilla extract
1 cup heavy cream
1 9-inch baked pie crust or crumb crust

In a medium bowl, sprinkle gelatin over 1 cup milk. Let stand for 5 minutes to soften gelatin. In a small saucepan, combine sugar and cocoa; add milk to mixture. Stir in corn syrup. Cook and stir over medium heat until mixture comes to a boil. Remove from heat. Add butter; stir until melted. Blend in remaining ¾ cup milk and vanilla. Pour into a large bowl. Cool to room temperature. Chill until almost set. In a separate bowl, whip cream until stiff. Beat chocolate gelatin on medium speed until smooth. Blend half of the whipped cream into the chocolate gelatin on low speed just until smooth. Pour into pie crust. Chill until set. Top with remaining whipped cream. Store in refrigerator.

Makes 8 servings

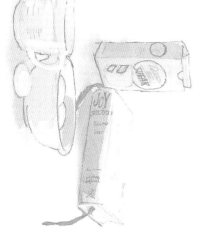

Old-Fashioned Pound Cake

2 cups butter
3½ cups granulated sugar
10 large or 12 small eggs
4 cups sifted all-purpose flour
1 teaspoon vanilla extract
Lemon Glaze (recipe follows)

Preheat oven to 300°F. Grease a 10-inch tube pan; set aside. In a large bowl, cream butter and sugar until light and fluffy. Add eggs, one at a time, beating well after each addition. Gradually add flour a cup at a time, blending well after each addition. Stir in vanilla; pour batter into prepared pan. Bake 2 hours or until a toothpick inserted near the center comes out clean. Cool in pan 10 minutes before turning out onto a wire rack to cool completely. Glaze with Lemon Glaze, if desired.

Makes 10 to 12 servings

Lemon Glaze

2 tablespoons butter or margarine, melted
4 teaspoons lemon juice
1 cup sifted confectioners' sugar

In a small bowl, combine butter and lemon juice. In a medium bowl, pour butter into confectioners' sugar; stir until smooth. Cool slightly.

Great-Grandma's Raisin Cake

1   teaspoon baking soda
1   cup boiling water
1   cup raisins
2   cups all-purpose flour
½   teaspoon baking powder
½   cup vegetable shortening
1   cup granulated sugar
1   egg
½   cup chopped nuts

Preheat oven to 350°F. Dissolve baking soda in boiling water and pour over raisins in a medium bowl; set aside to cool. In a large bowl, sift together flour and baking powder; set aside. In a separate bowl, cream shortening and sugar. Beat in egg; set aside. Stir raisin mixture into flour. Add creamed mixture; blend well. Stir in nuts. Spoon into a greased 9 x 5-inch loaf pan. Bake 60 minutes.

Makes 10 to 12 servings

Poppy Seed Cake

¼ cup poppy seeds
⅓ cup water
1 package white cake mix
2 egg whites

1 cups water
  Filling (recipe follows)
  Icing (recipe follows)

Pour ⅓ cup water over poppy seeds; let stand 30 minutes. Preheat oven to 350°F. In a large bowl, combine cake mix, poppy seed mixture, egg whites, and 1 cup water. Mix according to package directions. Pour into a greased and floured 9 x 13-inch baking pan. Bake 30 to 35 minutes. Cool cake; spread filling and top wth icing. Store in refrigerator.

Makes 12 servings

Filling

½ cup sour cream
2 egg yolks
¼ cup milk

1 3-ounce package instant vanilla
  pudding mix

In a small bowl, combine the first 3 ingredients. Stir in pudding mix. Spread on cooled cake.

Icing

¼ teaspoon cream of tartar
¼ teaspoon salt
2 egg whites, room
  temperature

¼ cup granulated sugar
¾ cup light corn syrup
1¼ teaspoons vanilla extract

In a large bowl, add cream of tartar and salt to egg whites; beat until soft peaks form. Gradually beat in sugar until smooth and glossy. Gradually add corn syrup and vanilla, beating until stiff peaks form, about 7 minutes.

Black Forest Cake

⅓ cup sifted all-purpose flour
⅓ cup cocoa
4 eggs
¾ teaspoon vanilla extract
⅔ cup granulated sugar
6 tablespoons clarified butter
½ cup granulated sugar
¾ cup water
¼ cup cherry juice
⅓ cup confectioners' sugar
2 cups heavy cream, whipped
1 cup pitted dark cherries, drained
1 4-ounce bar semisweet chocolate, shaved in curls
Maraschino cherries for garnish

Preheat oven to 350°F. In a small bowl, sift together flour and cocoa; set aside. In a large bowl, combine eggs, vanilla, and ⅔ cup sugar; beat 10 minutes at high speed. Fold flour into egg mixture. Add melted butter, stirring just until mixed. Do not overmix. Pour into 3 greased and floured 6-inch round pans. Bake 10 to 15 minutes. Cool in pans 5 minutes. Remove from pans and cool on racks.

In a saucepan, combine ½ cup sugar and water; boil 5 minutes. Cool to lukewarm and add cherry juice. Sprinkle over cake layers. Fold confectioners' sugar into whipped cream. Spread 1 cake layer with cream; sprinkle half the cherries on top. Repeat with second layer; add top layer. Frost top and sides of cake with remaining whipped cream; garnish with maraschino cherries and shaved chocolate. Store in refrigerator.

Makes 8 servings

Cola Cake

1 cup butter, softened
1⅓ cups granulated sugar
2 eggs
2 cups all-purpose flour
1 teaspoon baking soda
3 tablespoons cocoa
½ cup buttermilk
1 teaspoon vanilla extract
1 cup cola
1½ cups miniature marshmallows
  Cola Icing (recipe follows)

Preheat oven to 350°F. In a large bowl, cream butter and sugar until light and fluffy. Add eggs, one at a time, beating after each addition. In a separate bowl, sift together flour, baking soda, and cocoa; add to creamed mixture, alternating with buttermilk. Stir in vanilla and cola, blending well. Fold in marshmallows. Pour into a greased 9 x 13-inch baking pan. Bake 40 to 45 minutes. Cool and frost with Cola Icing.

Makes 12 servings

Cola Icing

4 cups confectioners' sugar
½ cup softened butter
3 tablespoons cocoa
⅓ cup cola
1 cup chopped pecans (optional)

In a large bowl, cream sugar, butter, and cocoa. Add cola, beating until smooth. Stir in pecans.

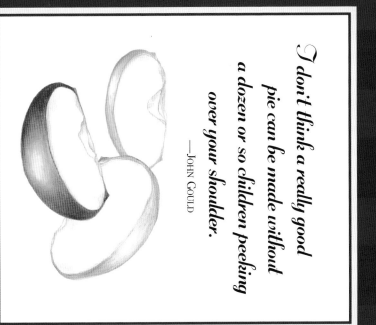

*I don't think a really good
pie can be made without
a dozen or so children peeking
over your shoulder.*

—JOHN GOULD

Holiday Chocolate Cake

2 cups granulated sugar
1¾ cups all-purpose flour
¾ cup cocoa
2 teaspoons baking soda
1 teaspoon baking powder
1 teaspoon salt
2 eggs
1 cup buttermilk or sour milk*
1 cup strong black coffee or 2 teaspoons instant coffee
   dissolved in 1 cup hot water
½ cup vegetable oil
2 teaspoons vanilla extract
Ricotta Cheese Filling (recipe follows)
Chocolate Whipped Cream Frosting (recipe follows)

Preheat oven to 350°F. In a large bowl, combine sugar, flour, cocoa, baking soda, baking powder, and salt. Add eggs, buttermilk or sour milk, coffee, oil, and vanilla; beat at medium speed for 2 minutes (batter will be thin). Pour into two greased and floured 9-inch round cake pans. Bake 30 to 35 minutes or until toothpick inserted into center comes out clean. Cool 10 minutes; remove from pans. Cool completely on wire racks.

Slice cake layers in half horizontally. Place bottom slice on serving plate; top with one-third of Ricotta Cheese Filling. Alternate cake layers and filling, ending with cake on top. Frost with Chocolate Whipped Cream Frosting. Store in refrigerator.

*To sour milk: Use 1 tablespoon vinegar plus milk to equal 1 cup.

Makes 8 to 10 servings

Ricotta Cheese Filling

1¾ cups ricotta cheese
¼ cup granulated sugar
3 tablespoons orange juice concentrate, undiluted
¼ cup candied red or green cherries, coarsely chopped
⅓ cup semi-sweet chocolate mini chips

In a small bowl, combine ricotta cheese, sugar, and orange juice concentrate; beat until smooth. Fold in candied fruit and mini chips.

Chocolate Whipped Cream Frosting

⅓ cup confectioners' sugar
2 tablespoons cocoa
1 cup heavy cream
1 teaspoon vanilla extract

In a small bowl, combine confectioners' sugar and cocoa. Add cream and vanilla; beat until stiff.

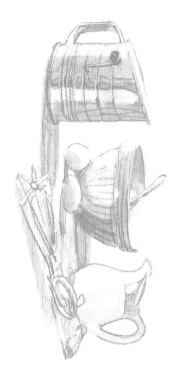

Strawberry-Topped Cheesecake

2 cups graham cracker crumbs
1¾ cups granulated sugar, divided
½ cup butter or margarine, melted
2 8-ounce packages cream cheese, softened
1 16-ounce container cream-style cottage cheese, sieved
2 teaspoons vanilla extract
½ teaspoon salt
6 eggs, separated
½ cup all-purpose flour
1 pint strawberries, hulled; reserve ½ cup for glaze
Strawberry Glaze (recipe follows)

Preheat oven to 350°F. In a large bowl, combine graham cracker crumbs, ¼ cup sugar, and butter; blend well. Press crumb mixture firmly into bottom and up sides of a 9-inch springform pan. Refrigerate until needed. In a large bowl, combine cheeses; beat until smooth. Blend in remaining 1½ cups sugar, vanilla, and salt. Add egg yolks, one at a time, beating well after each addition. Blend in flour. In a separate bowl, beat egg whites until stiff but not dry. Gently fold egg whites into cheese mixture. Pour into prepared pan. Bake 1½ hours. Turn off heat; open oven door and let cheesecake stand in oven at least 1 hour. Chill 3 to 4 hours before serving. Prepare Strawberry Glaze. Slice strawberries; arrange on top of cheesecake. Brush glaze over berries. Chill until glaze sets. Store in refrigerator.

Makes 10 to 12 servings

Strawberry Glaze

½ cup reserved strawberries, mashed
1 cup granulated sugar
¾ cup water, divided
2 tablespoons lemon juice
2 tablespoons cornstarch

Dissolve cornstarch in ¼ cup water. In a small saucepan, combine berries and sugar; add ½ cup water and lemon juice. Bring to a boil; reduce heat. Add cornstarch mixture to strawberries, stirring constantly until thickened. Remove from heat; strain and cool.

Double-Decker Espresso Mousse

1¼ cups granulated sugar, divided
⅓ cup cocoa
2 envelopes unflavored gelatin
2 cups cold espresso*
2 eggs, separated
1 teaspoon vanilla extract
1 8-ounce package cream cheese, softened
1 cup heavy cream
   Additional whipped cream
   Slivered orange peel, optional
   Chocolate curls, optional

In a saucepan, combine 1 cup sugar, cocoa, gelatin, and espresso. Beat egg yolks lightly; add to cocoa mixture. Cook over medium heat, stirring occasionally, until gelatin is dissolved and mixture is slightly thickened. Remove from heat; stir in vanilla. Cool to room temperature. In a large bowl, beat cream cheese. Add gelatin mixture; blend thoroughly. In a separate bowl, beat egg whites until foamy. Add remaining ¼ cup sugar, 1 tablespoon at a time, beating until soft peaks form. Beat heavy cream. Fold egg whites and whipped cream into gelatin mixture. Pour into a 1¼-quart serving bowl. Cover; chill several hours or overnight.

Unmold and serve with mounds of whipped cream spooned around the edge of the mousse. If desired, sprinkle with orange slivers and chocolate curls. Store in refrigerator.

*Espresso can be made by combining 2 tablespoons instant espresso coffee and 2 cups cold water.

Makes 10 to 12 servings

Cocoa Cream Puffs

1 tablespoon cocoa
1 cup water
1 tablespoon granulated sugar
⅛ teaspoon salt
7 tablespoons butter
1 cup sifted all-purpose flour
4 eggs
Cocoa Filling (recipe follows)
Whipped cream
Shaved chocolate

Preheat oven to 450°F. In a saucepan, combine cocoa, water, sugar, salt, and butter. Bring to a gentle boil, melting butter. Add flour, all at once. Stir quickly with a wooden spoon until batter leaves the sides of the pan. Remove from heat and cool slightly. Add eggs, one at a time, beating well after each addition. Dough will be smooth and glossy. If it is too soft, refrigerate 30 minutes. Butter baking sheet and drop dough in 12 mounds. Bake in a 450°F oven for 10 minutes. Reduce heat to 425°F and bake 10 minutes. Reduce heat to 400°F for 10 minutes. Remove from oven and cool 5 minutes. Turn off oven. Cut tops of puffs with a serrated knife and remove them. Return to oven 15 minutes, leaving door ajar. Remove and cool thoroughly. Fill with Cocoa Filling. Garnish with whipped cream and shaved chocolate. Store in refrigerator.

Makes 12 puffs

Cocoa Filling

1 cup semisweet chocolate chips
1 cup butterscotch chips
¼ cup milk
¼ cup granulated sugar
⅛ teaspoon salt
4 eggs, separated
1 teaspoon vanilla

In the top of a double boiler, combine chips, milk, sugar, and salt. Cook over hot water until mixture is smooth. Cool slightly. Add egg yolks, one at a time, beating well after each addition. Stir in vanilla. In a separate bowl, beat egg whites until stiff. Fold into chocolate mixture.

IDEALS FAVORITE FAMILY RECIPES

Chocolate Soufflé

4 eggs, separated
3 tablespoons butter
3 tablespoons all-purpose flour
1 cup milk
⅔ cup granulated sugar, divided
2 1-ounce squares semisweet chocolate
1½ teaspoons vanilla extract
¼ teaspoon salt

Preheat oven to 325°F. In a medium bowl, lightly beat the egg yolks; set aside. In a small saucepan, melt butter. Stir in flour; cook and stir until bubbly. Gradually add milk and ⅓ cup of sugar, stirring constantly until thickened. Add chocolate; stir until melted. Cool slightly; add chocolate mixture to egg yolks. Stir in vanilla; set aside. In a large bowl, beat egg whites and salt until foamy. Gradually add the remaining ⅓ cup sugar, beating until stiff peaks form. Fold chocolate mixture into egg whites. Turn into a 1½-quart casserole. Bake 60 to 75 minutes or until a knife inserted between center and outside edge comes out clean.

Makes 6 servings

Apricot Linzer Cookies

2 cups all-purpose flour
½ cup confectioners' sugar
¼ teaspoon baking soda
¼ cup ground almonds
¼ cup granulated sugar
½ cup butter, chilled and cut in 1-inch pieces
2 egg yolks, lightly beaten
½ teaspoon vanilla extract
¼ teaspoon cinnamon
1 egg, lightly beaten
½ cup apricot jam

Preheat oven to 350°F. In a large bowl, combine flour, confectioners' sugar, and baking soda. Stir in almonds and granulated sugar. Cut in butter with a pastry blender or two knives until mixture resembles coarse crumbs. Add egg yolks, vanilla, and cinnamon; blend well. Gather dough into a ball. Turn out onto a lightly floured board. Knead lightly; shape into a smooth ball. Roll out dough to ¼-inch thickness. Cut out cookies with a floured 2-inch round cookie cutter. With a floured thimble, cut holes in centers of half of the cookies. Brush all the cookies with beaten egg. Place on a greased baking sheet. Bake 18 minutes or until golden brown. Remove from baking sheet to a wire rack to cool. When cool, spread jam on whole cookies. Top each with a cut-out cookie.

Makes about 1½ dozen

Hazelnut Macaroons

8 egg whites
⅛ teaspoon cream of tartar
2½ cups granulated sugar
½ teaspoon vanilla extract
1 pound ground hazelnuts

In a large bowl, beat egg whites and cream of tartar until foamy. Gradually add sugar, beating until stiff peaks form. Blend in vanilla. Fold in hazelnuts. Cover and chill 2 hours.

Preheat oven to 300°F. Line a 10 x 15-inch baking sheet with parchment paper; drop batter by teaspoonfuls onto baking sheet. Bake 1 hour or until golden brown. Remove from baking sheet to a wire rack to cool.

Makes about 7 dozen

In addition to hazelnuts, macaroons can be made with almonds or coconut. Flavorings such as chocolate or vanilla can also be added.

Almond Butter Cookies

1 cup butter, softened
3 tablespoons granulated sugar
1 teaspoon almond extract
2 cups all-purpose flour
½ teaspoon salt
Sliced, unblanched almonds
Powdered Sugar Frosting (recipe follows)

In a large bowl, cream butter and sugar until light and fluffy. Blend in almond extract. In a separate bowl, stir together flour and salt. Gradually add flour mixture to creamed mixture; blend well. Cover and chill until firm. Preheat oven to 400°F. Shape dough into ¾-inch balls. Place on ungreased baking sheet. With the bottom of a glass dipped in flour, flatten balls to ¼-inch thickness. Bake 5 to 6 minutes. Remove from baking sheet to a wire rack to cool. Spread about ½ teaspoon frosting on each cookie. Top with a sliced almond.

Makes about 5 dozen

Powdered Sugar Frosting

1 cup sifted confectioners' sugar
1 tablespoon butter, softened
½ teaspoon vanilla extract
1½ tablespoons hot water

In a small bowl, combine sugar, butter, and vanilla; blend well. Add water; beat until of spreading consistency.

Pinwheel Cookies

½ cup butter or margarine, softened
1 3-ounce package cream cheese, softened
1 cup granulated sugar
1 egg
1 teaspoon vanilla extract
2¼ cups all-purpose flour, divided
½ teaspoon baking powder
½ teaspoon salt
⅛ teaspoon baking soda
½ cup cocoa

In a large bowl, cream butter, cream cheese, sugar, egg, and vanilla until light and fluffy. In a separate bowl, sift together 1½ cups flour, baking powder, salt, and baking soda; blend into creamed mixture. Divide dough in half. Add cocoa to one half of dough; blend well. Add ¾ cup flour to remaining half of dough; blend well. On a lightly floured board, roll out each half into a 9-inch square. (If dough is too soft, chill about 15 minutes.) Place chocolate dough on top of vanilla. Roll up jelly-roll style. Wrap tightly in waxed paper; chill several hours or overnight.

Preheat oven to 350°F. Slice dough ¼ inch thick. Place on an ungreased baking sheet. Bake 12 to 15 minutes or until lightly browned. Remove from cookie sheet; cool on wire rack.

Makes about 3 dozen

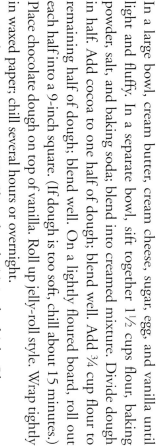

Favorite Brownies

Cream Cheese Filling (recipe follows)

½ cup butter
⅓ cup cocoa
2 eggs
1 cup granulated sugar
1 teaspoon vanilla
½ cup all-purpose flour
½ teaspoon baking powder
¼ teaspoon salt
½ cup chopped nuts, optional
Brownie Frosting (recipe follows)

Preheat oven to 350°F. Prepare Cream Cheese Filling; set aside. In a small saucepan, melt butter. Remove from heat; stir in cocoa. In a large bowl, beat eggs until foamy. Gradually add sugar and vanilla; blend well. Stir in flour, baking powder, and salt. Add chocolate mixture and nuts; mix well. Spread half of chocolate batter in a greased 9-inch square pan. Spread Cream Cheese Filling over chocolate. Drop spoonfuls of remaining chocolate batter onto cream cheese layer. Use a knife or spatula to gently swirl chocolate batter into cream cheese layer for a marbled effect. Bake 40 to 50 minutes or until brownie springs back when lightly touched in center. Cool completely in pan. Frost with Brownie Frosting. Cut into squares.

Makes about 16 brownies

Cream Cheese Filling

1   3-ounce package cream cheese, softened
2   tablespoons butter or margarine, softened
¼   cup granulated sugar
1   egg, slightly beaten
1   tablespoon all-purpose flour
½   teaspoon vanilla extract

In a medium bowl, blend cream cheese and butter. Add sugar; beat until fluffy. Add egg, flour, and vanilla; blend well.

Brownie Frosting

3   tablespoons butter or margarine
3   tablespoons cocoa
1   teaspoon vanilla extract
1   cup confectioners' sugar
1   to 2 tablespoons milk

In a medium bowl, blend butter, cocoa, and vanilla. Add confectioners' sugar and 1 tablespoon of the milk. Gradually beat in remaining 1 tablespoon milk.

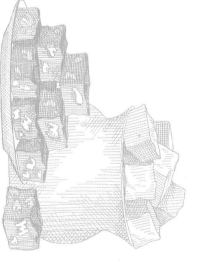

Index

Almond Butter Cookies, 156
Applesauce Nut Bread, 30
Apricot Linzer Cookies, 154
Aunt Dessy's Moussaka, 110
Baked Sauerkraut, 52
Baked Stuffed Salmon, 89
Banana Muffins, 33
Beef Stroganoff, 102
Black Forest Cake, 145
Brunswick Stew, 62
Buttermilk Biscuits, 34
Buttermilk Pancakes, 117
Carrot & Raisin Salad, 39
Cheese & Spinach Appetizers, 14
Cheesy Surprise Bread, 25
Chicken & Dumplings, 103
Chicken Fricassee, 91
Chicken Gumbo, 63
Chicken Liver Pâté, 11
Chicken Noodle Skillet Dinner, 104
Chicken Paprika Casserole, 105
Chicken Pie, 92
Chili con Carne, 66
Chocolate Bavarian Cream Pie, 141
Chocolate Soufflé, 153
Cinnamon Coffee Round, 29
Classic Cioppino, 72
Cocoa Cream Puffs, 152
Cola Cake, 146
Cornish Game Hens with Wild Rice, 94
Country Corn Bread, 36
Crabmeat Rounds, 18
Crab-Stuffed Mushrooms, 18
Cream of Potato Soup, 55
Creamed Spinach, 44
Creamed Turkey with Popovers, 107
Creamy Asparagus Casserole, 43
Creamy Cheese Ball, 12
Cucumber-Cheese Sandwiches, 9
Curried Lamb, 81
Deep-Dish Strawberry-Rhubarb Pie, 140
Deluxe Potato Salad, 40
Double-Decker Espresso Mousse, 151
Easy Egg & Sausage Casserole, 123
Easy Morning Omelet, 119
Eggs Benedict, 122

Egg-Salad Stuffed Tomatoes, 132
Favorite Brownies, 158
Favorite Onion Soup, 56
Favorite Yeast Rolls, 27
Fish Stew, 71
Fresh Corn Pudding, 45
Garden Skillet Stew, 61
Gazpacho Macaroni Salad, 133
Glazed Baby Carrots, 44
Glazed Fruit Tarts, 137
Golden Hash Browns, 118
Grandma's White Bread, 22
Great Baked Beans, 48
Great-Grandma's Raisin Cake, 143
Ham Bone Soup, 68
Ham Deviled Eggs, 17
Ham Pinwheels, 17
Hazelnut Macaroons, 155
Hearty Bean Soup, 59
Holiday Chocolate Cake, 148
Homestyle Gingerbread, 31
Homestyle Macaroni & Cheese, 97
Homestyle Potato Pancakes, 118
Hungarian Goulash, 101
Hush Puppies, 36
Irish Soda Bread, 24
Jambalaya, 65
Lamb Spanakopita, 80
Lemon Meringue Pie, 139
Lentil Soup, 58
Mashed Rutabagas & Potatoes, 50
Minestrone with Sausage, 69
Miniature Cream Puffs, 134
Mixed Vegetable Soup, 57
Mulligatawny Soup, 67
New Orleans Gumbo, 70
Nutty Date Bread, 32
Old-Fashioned Doughnuts, 129
Old-Fashioned Oatmeal Bread, 21
Old-Fashioned Pound Cake, 142
Old-Fashioned Stuffed Cabbage, 113
Old-Time Fish & Chips, 88
One-Pot Lamb Roast, 98
Onion & Bacon Quiche, 125
Oven-Barbecued Spareribs, 86
Oven-Roasted Potatoes, 49

Peachy-Plum Fritters, 128
Pecan Chess Pie, 140
Perfect Peach Crisp, 138
Pineapple Cheese Ball, 11
Pineapple Waldorf, 131
Pinwheel Cookies, 157
Poached Eggs Florentine, 121
Poppy Seed Cake, 144
Pork Roast with Herb Stuffing, 84
Puffy Cheese Appetizers, 13
Raisin Braid, 23
Salisbury Steak Dinner, 78
Saucy Meat Loaf, 75
Sausage Quiche, 124
Savory Black-Eyed Peas, 46
Scalloped Potatoes, 49
Scalloped Potatoes & Ham, 114
Seven-Layer Salad, 39
Shepherd's Pie, 79
Southern Fried Chicken, 93
South-of-the-Border Omelet, 120
Stewed Okra & Tomatoes, 42
Sticky Pecan Rolls, 26
Strawberry Cream Crepes, 130
Strawberry-Topped Cheesecake, 150
Stuffed Celery, 9
Stuffed Grape Leaves, 82
Stuffed Green Peppers, 112
Stuffed Round Steak, 76
Stuffed Shells, 111
Stuffed Tiny Tomatoes, 10
Sunday Baked Ham, 87
Swedish Red Cabbage, 52
Sweet & Spicy Meatballs, 16
Sweet Potato Biscuits, 35
Sweet Potato Casserole, 51
Taco Casserole, 100
Tamale Cheese Pie, 90
Texas Coleslaw, 41
Turkey Tetrazzini, 106
Uncle Tony's Lasagna, 109
Winter Vegetable Stew, 60
Yankee Pot Roast, 99
Zucchini & Tomato Casserole, 42
Zucchini Frittata, 126